Guitars from George & Leo

How Leo Fender and I Built G&L Guitars

by George Fullerton

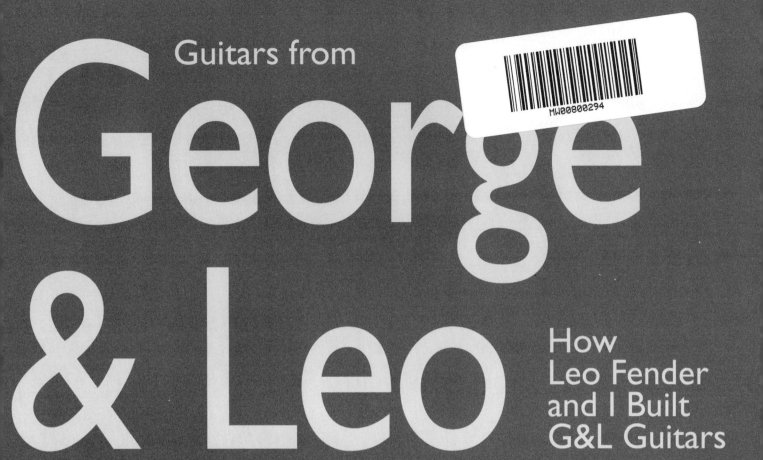

ISBN 0-634-06922-5

Stratocaster, Strat, Tele, and Telecaster are registered trademarks of Fender Musical Instruments Corporation

In Australia Contact:
Hal Leonard Australia Pty. Ltd.
22 Taunton Drive   P.O. Box 5130
Cheltenham East, 3192   Victoria, Australia
Email: ausadmin@halleonard.com

Published by Hal Leonard Corporation
7777 W. Bluemound Road
P.O. Box 13819
Milwaukee, WI 53213

Library of Congress Cataloging-in Publication Data has been applied for.

Printed in U.S.A.
First Edition

Visit Hal Leonard Online at
www.halleonard.com

Contents

Foreword: by Tim Page v

Preface: by Rick "Shorty" Robins vii

Preface: by Will Ray viii

Introduction: by George Fullerton xi

Acknowledgments xii

PART I—Founding Fender and G&L 1

Chapter 1—My Move to Orange County 3

Chapter 2—Leo's Early Life and Businesses 6

Chapter 3—A New Beginning 17

Chapter 4—Building the Broadcaster 20

Chapter 5—Creating the Precision Bass 25

Chapter 6—Developing the Stratocaster Guitar 28

Chapter 7— The Jazzmaster and Color Bursts on the Scene.......31

Chapter 8—Innovation Continues 34

Color Photo Gallery

The "(PG)" in the captions of any black and white photo indicates that the photo also appears in the color section.

Chapter 9—CBS Buys Fender, Sells Fender 37

Chapter 10—Leo's Life After Fender 44

Chapter 11—The Founding of CLF Research Corp. and MusicMan........47

PART II—Building G&L and the G&L Way 55

Chapter 12— G&L Musical Products Inc. Comes on the Scene.................57

Chapter 13— G&L Takes Hold, Leo Lets Go 60

Chapter 14—BBE Sound Buys G&L 65

Chapter 15—Building a G&L 71

Chapter 16—Making Body Blanks 73

Chapter 17—Making Instrument Necks 79

Chapter 18—Putting the Finish On 86

Chapter 19—Building Great Pickups 91

Chapter 20—Gathering Other Parts, Entering Final Assembly.................95

PART III—A Detailed History of G&L Instruments 103

Chapter 21—The First G&L Guitars and Basses 105

Chapter 22—The Innovative G-200 107

Chapter 23—The Evolution of the S-500 109

Chapter 24—The ASAT 113

Chapter 25—G&L Rock Guitars 119

Chapter 26—SC and HG Models: The Student Range 122

Chapter 27—G&L Basses in the '80s 124

Chapter 28—G&L in the '90s: The Second Decade 127

Chapter 29—Evolution of the ASAT 129

Chapter 30—Evolution of the S-500 and Comanche 134

Chapter 31—Evolution of G&L Rock Guitars 137

Chapter 32—G&L Basses in the '90s 139

Chapter 33—Creating the Custom Creations Department......................144

Chapter 34—G&L in the New Millennium 147

Chapter 35—Distinctive G&L Features...151

PART IV—Favorite Players and Entertainers 155

Chapter 36—The Importance of Classic Cowboys...................................157

Chapter 37—Contemporary Country Musicians 165

Chapter 38—Travel Tales...170

PART V—Remembering Leo and Recollecting More G&L Details 183

Chapter 39—Leo's Legacy 185

Foreword

When George asked if I would write the foreword to his new book about G&L guitars, I was deeply honored. George's life has crossed paths with some of the most famous musicians and people of our time, so why he chose me left me speechless.

Most of all, I was excited by the information he had written. For those of us who collect and play G&L instruments, it was an opportunity to learn more about the innovations that make the G&Ls sought by players everywhere. It also puts the story down in the history books from the "G" in G&L: George Fullerton, Leo Fender's lifelong business partner and best friend. You can't get much better than that.

As first, I felt this foreword should reflect the historical accomplishments of George and Leo. But after tossing around several variations, I realized the only way to truly write a foreword about G&L would be to speak with the passion and love I have for the instruments as both a player and as a dealer.

G&L guitars are the best, period. There isn't a guitar for the dollar or even several dollars more that comes close to touching the value they offer. There isn't a need to find a boutique manufacturer who "makes them like they used to." Why? Because G&L does make them like they used to.

If you were to visit the G&L factory on Fender Ave. today, you would think you just walked out of a time machine into 1955. In this day and age of computer-aided construction and CNC machines, you won't find them at G&L. Instead, you see human beings building instruments by hand—winding pickups, shaping necks, painting bodies, and putting in that "soul" which is so often lost in mass-produced instruments.

I'm impressed that the majority of the people at G&L are musicians—just like you, me, and everyone who has ever bought a G&L. They know what a guitar should feel like. You can watch as a worker makes a neck. He stops to hold it like he's playing, and just by feel, knows it needs a bit more sanding here or shaping there. You don't get that in a stamp-them-out-as-fast-as-possible plant. The result is that each G&L has its own personality.

It's not a question of whether one brand is better than another. G&L is the logical evolution of what George and Leo would have done had Leo never sold Fender to CBS back in 1965. The Magnetic Field Design pickups are phenomenal. The Dual-Fulcrum vibrato system is flawless. George's design of the three-bolt neck is perfect. The Saddle-Lock bridge is simply the best in the industry. If you want sustain, buy a G&L.

Leo said, "G&L guitars are the best instruments I've ever made." And Leo meant it. George said, "My partner and I made the world's most famous guitar, then we set out to make the best." And George was right.

These two men not only made their mark on this world, but carved it in stone. If you want that feel, that sound, you'll find both in a G&L. It's the musician's instrument, and it's still made in Fullerton under the watchful eyes and spirit of George and Leo in a company called G&L.

Thank you, George, and thank you, Leo.

Tim Page
Buffalo Brothers Guitars
Carlsbad, California

Preface

The most memorable experience in my life was my association and friendship with George Fullerton and Leo Fender. They are truly legends in the eyes of the world and pioneers in the guitar and music industry; but to me they will always be special friends that I will never forget.

George made it possible for me to be a part of the Fender guitar family, and it truly was like a family. I was with the Fender Company during the good old days—in the early '60s—before and after CBS. I worked there for about seven years, before going into country music as a full-time performer. I will always look back with gratitude to the time when, after my guitar was stolen, George and Leo helped me build my dream guitar: a black G&L Broadcaster. I still play it and always will.

Even years after I left the Fender Co., I often spent time with George and Leo, both during the MusicMan days and until Leo passed away. I really enjoyed our visits and lunches together. I miss those days very much, and I feel privileged to have been a part of the legend and legacy of George Fullerton and Leo Fender.

Rick "Shorty" Robins

Preface

I first became interested in G&L guitars in the early days of The Hellecasters, when fellow band mate John Jorgenson let me pick up his ASAT Special during a break in rehearsals one day.

I was immediately struck by the clear yet ballsy tone it projected. My guitar at that time was a Frankenstein affair, with the neck, body, pickups, and bridge all made by different manufacturers. After that rehearsal I immediately set up a meeting with the G&L Artist Relations representative in Fullerton. When I arrived I found a couple of stock ASAT Specials laying around in his office, so I casually picked one up and played it through a small amp he had. I couldn't believe how well the factory guys had set up the guitar. The body was nice and light, the neck was incredibly comfortable, the action was just right, the bridge intonated perfectly, and the two MFD pickups were very responsive and clear. I picked up the other ASAT and found the same thing. I was really impressed. He told me to take one of them home and "mess around with it." So I did.

When I got it home, I found myself strangely unable to put it down. It was like my fingers refused to let me go to bed. After playing it most of the night I knew this guitar wasn't going back to that rep. I would do whatever had to be done to hold on to it. A few days later I took it to a rehearsal for a band I had been producing and playing with, Wylie & the Wild West Show. I was intrigued with how "hi fi" the pickups sounded through my amp—rich low end, fat middles, and a sizzling top. Even the band noticed how much fuller my sound was over my old guitar, which now seemed very "lo fi" to me by comparison. From that moment on, I became a true believer and have never looked back. Since then I have owned Comanches, Legacys, ASAT Classics, Z-3s, and a few years ago was honored with my own G&L signature model.

As a musician who has owned and played hundreds of guitars in my lifetime, I am still in awe of the many guitar innovations that Leo Fender and George Fullerton have made at G&L. The necks are rock solid and never seem to warp under the battle conditions of touring. The fingerboards always fit my hands comfortably, and the large 6100 frets are just right for my country and blues bending. The MFD pickups using ceramic magnets are light years ahead of the competition, able to go from a whisper to a roar at the drop of a pick. The hum cancelling Z coil pickups used on the Z-3s and Comanches are, in my humble opinion, one of the greatest advances ever developed for the electric guitar. These full range pickups are much more musical than traditional humbuckers and are absolutely dead quiet on noisy stages or around unshielded studio computer monitors.

Another G&L innovation is the Saddle-Lock bridge used on ASAT Specials and Z-3s. These are without a doubt the best bridges ever made for a solid-body guitar. Not only do they intonate accurately and sustain for days, but I also break fewer strings because of the gentler angle of the strings traveling over the saddles. Ask any guitar player what his biggest fear is and he'll probably tell you it's breaking a string right in the middle of a hot solo. Fewer string changes are needed, which means fewer hassles for musicians. I've been playing G&Ls now for many years and can safely say that these are the best and most consistently made electric guitars I have ever owned, bar none. Yes, Virginia, they still make guitars by hand in Fullerton.

Will Ray

Introduction

My first book, *Guitar Legends*, was about my association with Leo Fender. It covered the time we met and how we got started designing and manufacturing electric guitars and basses.

We were the first to design and produce a solid-body electric guitar. That instrument was the beginning of the fabulous Fender Electric Instrument Co. We built on that experience and ultimately founded G&L Musical Products, Inc. Our goal was to have the ultimate line of instruments with our latest and best designs. The G&L line is the pinnacle of our achievement.

This book, *Guitars by George & Leo*, amplifies what is in the first book by discussing the founding of G&L, detailing all the G&L instruments, and covering the importance of G&L to the music industry.

"G&L" stands for George and Leo. Given Leo's incredible prominence, I have been asked many times why my name had top billing. After discussing several different names for the company, Leo said, "The name I want for the new company is G&L."

I felt honored to have this position in the final company that Leo and I built together. Being in the electric instrument business has been a satisfying adventure for both of us. Leo and I had some wonderful years working at the various companies, from Fender to MusicMan to G&L.

This is not just another guitar book like so many others. It is about the people who build musical instruments and the musicians who play them. Part IV covers some of the interesting characters Leo and I met, including some silver screen idols. Also included are many country, rock, blues, and gospel groups who are part of the music heritage that is vital to this great nation.

Many people played a part in the development and success of the electric guitar and bass. The importance of those instruments to the music industry and show business cannot be overstated. It's my hope that this book pays tribute to the people and the instruments because of the many good things in life they bring.

George Fullerton
Fullerton, California

Acknowledgements

I'm very grateful to and appreciative of the many wonderful people who have helped Leo Fender and me to make our combined ideas a reality and in building great guitars and basses.

Also to the many musicians and music lovers all over the world, who buy, use, and love the sound and quality of G&L instruments.

I give special thanks to John McLaren, CEO and Chairman of the Board of BBE Sound—who purchased the G&L Company after Leo Fender passed away—for his time and effort in providing encouragement in writing this book

Thanks to David McLaren for his help in getting the needed information about all of the G&L instruments built since the beginning, and also for the many pictures he submitted for the book.

Thanks to Tim Page of Buffalo Brothers for his time and energy in locating the many pictures, and for his gathering of other informative material used in this book.

I thank Robb Lawrence for the helpful information he provided about different instruments, and the pictures he provided for the book.

Thanks to Janis Rizzuto, who did a very fine job of editing this manuscript.

Thanks to Amy Lomusio for the computer work she did on the manuscript.

Finally, to my wife Lucille, who stood by me with patience while all of the work on this book was being done. I love you.

PART I
Founding Fender and G&L

Chapter 1

My Move to Orange County

In the early 1940s, the Los Angeles area was growing quickly due to the influx of people from all over the United States. These people sought employment in the high-paying government defense industry. Many built airplanes and other equipment to support the war effort.

I decided to move to California during this boom time. I was planning to pursue a career in electronics. However, finding a place to live posed a problem not only for me, but for others as well. There was a tremendous shortage of rental property and rents were high.

I wanted an alternative. The Orange County area, southeast of Los Angeles, was less crowded and had more of a small-town atmosphere. To me, it was a more acceptable and affordable place to live and work.

To find the different lifestyle I sought, I traveled around to some of the smaller towns to see what they had to offer. A friend and I decided to drive around the countryside to see and enjoy the various places that dotted the county. The main highway to Orange County was California State Highway 101.

Snowcapped mountains, from Mount Baldy, east to Big Bear

Highway 101 passes through Los Angeles and winds its way southeast through rolling hills. The view along this highway was magnificent, with the San Gabriel and San Bernardino mountain ranges on the north, stretching from Mount Baldy east to Big Bear. They still had their snow-covered tops showing brightly in the strong morning sunlight.

This time was long before freeways and blacktop parking lots, as well as before thousands of houses were built. Instead, there was clear, fresh air and no smog.

As we continued to travel, a sign by the roadside informed us that we were leaving Los Angeles County and entering Orange County. The scenery was beginning to change. I distinctly remember one sign along the road. It was a green bell hanging high on a curved pole. The sign underneath said "El Camino Real," which means "The King's Highway."

El Camino Real connects California's 21 Spanish Missions from San Diego to Sonoma, a distance of more than 500 miles. It passes through several beautiful towns with interesting historical sites.

El Camino Real follows old Indian trails and some of the original dirt roadways, which have long since been paved. The special markers were established in 1906, and some of these signs can still be seen today.

Continuing further into Orange County, we could see that much of the countryside was covered with orange trees, branches heavy with fruit. As we traveled on, we encountered an overhead bridge for trains to pass over the roadway. On this beautiful white arched bridge was a message in black letters, "Welcome to Fullerton." After passing under the bridge, the road became Spadra Road, which was the north to south main drag through the small town of Fullerton, Calif.

"El Camino Real" ("The King's Highway")
sign on mission bell pole.

The welcome sign for travelers entering Fullerton, California.

Orange trees—California gold.

At the time, Fullerton had a population of about 9,000 people. It was considered the center of the orange growing industry. Many of its residents were focused on producing top-quality oranges, which required a great deal of attention and careful handling. The trees had to be fertilized, sprayed, and watered to promote healthy growth. When cold weather came there was concern for keeping the fruit from freezing. Smudge pots had to be placed in between the rows of trees and lighted at night to warm the air and prevent freezing. These smudge pots burned oil and produced a dark pall of smoke that stayed almost all day after a cold night in the groves.

South of Fullerton a few miles was Anaheim, another small town. In later years, Highway 101's name would be changed to Anaheim Blvd., which would become the main north-to-south thoroughfare through town. One of the main streets running east to west was called La Palma Ave. This was a busy area for the fruit and walnut growing industry.

At the time, I didn't realize the impact this area and its people would have on my future. Who would have dreamed Fullerton would become "The Guitar Capital of the World."

Chapter 2

Leo's Early Life and Businesses

Soon after the turn of the century, Clarence "Monte" Fender left his native Illinois and moved to Montana. He did not remain in Montana long before he decided to move to Southern California.

Clarence moved first to Anaheim and later north to San Luis Obispo. While living there, he met his wife-to-be, Harriet Wood. They were married Jan.15, 1907, in San Luis Obispo. Later that year, they moved back to Anaheim, where they bought some land on La Palma Ave. and began the process of planting an orange grove.

Clarence "Monte" and Harriet Fender:
Leo's father and mother.

A copy of the marriage license for Leo Fender's father and mother.

"This Lone Oak Tree";
This lone oak tree is the only visible thing left
of the Fender family Lone Oak Ranch.

They called this land "The Lone Oak Ranch" because there was just a single oak tree on the property. Their plan was to live here and work hard to get the grove planted, with the hopes of reaping a good income when the orchard produced fruit.

However, developing an orchard requires a lot of time, effort, and money. But Clarence and Harriet only had a limited amount of money, and there were no buildings on the property. To use this place as a home and working ranch, they

Fender family house on Lone Oak Ranch, 1951.

Barn on Lone Oak Ranch.
Family lived in barn where Leo Fender was born.
Baby in picture is Leo Fender.

The Fender family home built on the Lone Oak Ranch in Anaheim, California.

needed some sort of structure. So they erected a large barn, and divided it in two. One side was used for things necessary for the ranch and its animals. The other half became living quarters.

During this time, the family struggled to make ends meet. For cash, Clarence grew small patches of vegetables. When the produce was harvested, he took it by wagon to an area near Newport Beach, called the Anaheim Landing, to be sold to the public. He also earned money by hauling manure from nearby dairies and delivering it to orange growers for fertilizer. To get everything accomplished, Clarence started his day before daylight and ended it after dark.

Harriet also had a job. She supervised the workings of a nearby walnut grove. This was a big responsibility since she had to learn Spanish in order to communicate with the farm workers and others involved in the growing, harvesting, and packing of the walnuts.

On Aug. 10, 1909, a baby boy was born into the family. His name was Clarence Leo Fender. A baby girl, Wilda, was born later.

Leo Fender's high school graduation picture.

Leo's sister: Wilda Fender's high school graduation picture.

Many years passed. Leo went to high school in Fullerton, where he attained high honors. He and Wilda both graduated from Fullerton High School. After high school, he attended California State University at Long Beach.

Leo worked at various jobs during high school and college. One of these jobs was delivering ice. After doing this hard work, he decided there must be an easier way to make a living.

Leo's inquisitive mind and inventive nature lead him to several different careers. After graduation, he became an accountant for the state of California, working in San Luis Obispo. According to his sister Wilda Gray, he was married in 1934 to Esther Klotzly.

Newspaper announcement of the wedding of Leo Fender and Esther Klotzly in 1934.

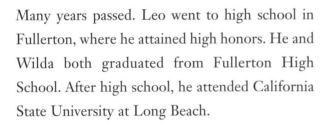

Clarence Fender Wed Fullerton Girl This Morning

At a strictly simple and informal wedding at 7 o'clock this morning, Miss Esther May Klotzly of Fullerton, daughter of Mr. and Mrs. E. E. Klotzly, also of that city, became the bride of Clarence L. Fender, son of Mr. and Mrs. C. M. Fender, West La Palma, Anaheim.

The wedding service was read by the Rev. George F. Tinsley, pastor of the Fullerton Christian church, at the parish house in the presence of members of the immediate families of the two young people.

Both bride and bridegroom were unattended, while the bride chose for her wedding ensemble a smart suit of sea green silk which was trimmed with white fur, matching her large white hat and other white accessories.

Following the pledging of the marriage vows, the new Mr. and Mrs. Fender departed immediately for a honeymoon trip to the north.

Upon their return to the southland they will be at home to their friends at the new home at 309 Marwood avenue, Fullerton.

Both Mr. and Mrs. Fender are graduates of the Fullerton schools.

Mr. Fender is in business for himself at the Fender Radio service in Anaheim.

This building at 107 S. Spadra (now Harbor Blvd.) where Leo had his first radio repair business. He also built his first lap steel guitars and amps with Doc Kauffman in the back room.

Front and back view of a small radio designed and built by Leo Fender in 1945. Never produced.

When the job with the state became slow and monotonous, Leo became discouraged. He wanted to get into the electronics field, which he had studied while in college. He left his job and returned to Fullerton. He started a business repairing radios, but struggled to find a place to perform the work. After using several unsuitable places, he got a small shop that was converted from a house. It was located on Spadra Road.

Unfortunately, the shop was on low ground at the edge of an orange grove, which was subject to flooding in the heavy rainy season. And in 1938, there was a terrible storm. Leo's building was caught in the flooding water and washed away. This put Leo in the difficult situation of trying to get his business started again. After a couple of years, he was able to rent a small building in downtown Fullerton.

It was rough going. The war effort had taken just about every available electronic item needed for radio repair. But Leo was able to get along on parts salvaged from a supplier's junk heap. Still, the business kept him busy, and he was able to bring in enough money to pay the bills and living expenses.

During this time, Leo became interested in designing magnetic pickups for guitars. Musicians wanted pickups mounted on their guitars, so the instruments could be heard better and stand out in the band. Recording studios also liked the idea of being able to hear the guitar more clearly in recordings.

Leo was able to design a pickup that could be mounted permanently into an opening cut into the top of a hollow-body guitar. This product brought him some better income. He did all the work himself—from winding the coils to make the pickups to installing them in customers' guitars.

He continued making and installing pickups for customers, all the while thinking about creating other electronic products. One of his early ideas was to design and build small radios. That venture did not go well and only a few were produced. Another more successful plan was to design and build amplifiers for players to use with their new electric guitar pickups. From there, he built a lap steel guitar, also known as a Hawaiian, and a small amplifier to create a matching set. This product benefited from the popularity of Hawaiian music at the time.

After operating in the small building for a while, Leo realized he needed more space to do his work and expand his business. The Melody Inn, a restaurant across the street at 107 S. Spadra Road, was also seeking to expand. Initially, the owners considered renting the building next to Leo, but it was not quite large enough for their expansion plans. But Leo's space and the one next to it would be ample room for their new restaurant. So they started the process of trading buildings with Leo.

Leo now had the space needed for repairing radios, winding coils, and making pickups. He also had room in the front of his store to sell items such as small radios, phonograph records, sheet music, and songbooks. This led him to become more interested in designing and building single-neck steel guitars and amplifiers.

Leo's partner in this venture was C.O. "Doc" Kauffman, whom he had met several years before when Doc had a repair shop on Commonwealth

Ave. in Fullerton. This new venture was called K and F Instruments. It was housed in a garage in back of Leo's store that they converted into a small factory. By working long hours and weekends, these two inventive and talented men were able to get this business going in a short time.

K&F early-day amplifiers, 1946.
Front view

Back view

Doc Kauffman and Leo Fender with early-day lap steel guitars.

Sometimes they would work until midnight, building workbenches and tooling for new instruments. Most of their equipment was handmade. They funded their venture with money they got after selling a license for a phonograph record changer they designed for Voice of Music in Benton Harbor, Mich.

In addition to working on the steel guitars, they worked together designing magnetic pickups for guitars. They spent quite a lot of time searching out different methods for winding coils with various sizes and shapes of coil forms. One of these forms had an open center, with the coil wire wound around the outside. This coil was mounted between two metal plates, with one on top of the winding. The bottom plate had a special shape on the back edge that became the bridge of the guitar with the strings passing through the opening in the coil form. These two metal plates had two fairly large magnets that held the plates together, along with two long machine screws that held the pickup unit on a base plate. The base plate had some slotted holes in it where the machine screws passed through. These slotted holes permitted the pickups to be moved either way to adjust the string length for proper string intonation.

The steel guitar and amplifier business grew quickly. Soon Leo and Doc had several people working for them. Besides the steel guitar and amplifiers, they built amplifiers in other sizes. Some were painted with gray crinkled finish on the cabinets and others had cabinets in natural maple or black walnut. These amplifiers were made with multi-colored grill cloth and had a matching back panel.

During this time they received a request to build a high-output amplifier. That was when they

K&F amplifier and lap steel guitar: first of six sets built by Leo Fender and Doc Kauffman, about 1944.

Special guitar neck handmade by Doc Kauffman. Doc gave this neck to me; I have it in my collection.

This K&F amp with top-mount chassis was the first built with hanging tubes; this method became the standard for the industry, 1945.

Photos courtesy of Ken Kauffman

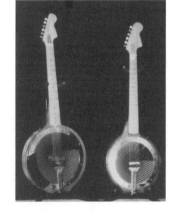

Some of Doc Kauffman's musical instruments

started to design the push pull 6L6-tube unit. Doc says he asked Leo to hang the chassis upside down in the top of the cabinet. Eventually this design was used on all Fender amplifiers. It became the famous Fender Dual Amplifier with the slanted front on the cabinet and chrome strip between the twin 10-inch Jensen speakers.

Again, the business quickly outgrew the building. So Leo bought a lot a few blocks from the store on the corner of Pomona and Santa Fe Avenues in Fullerton. Leo was having new metal buildings

built at the site. He was pressing to get Doc interested in making this expensive move to the new buildings and to move the manufacturing part of the business to this location.

Doc was reluctant to get involved any deeper. He realized the amount of money it would take to

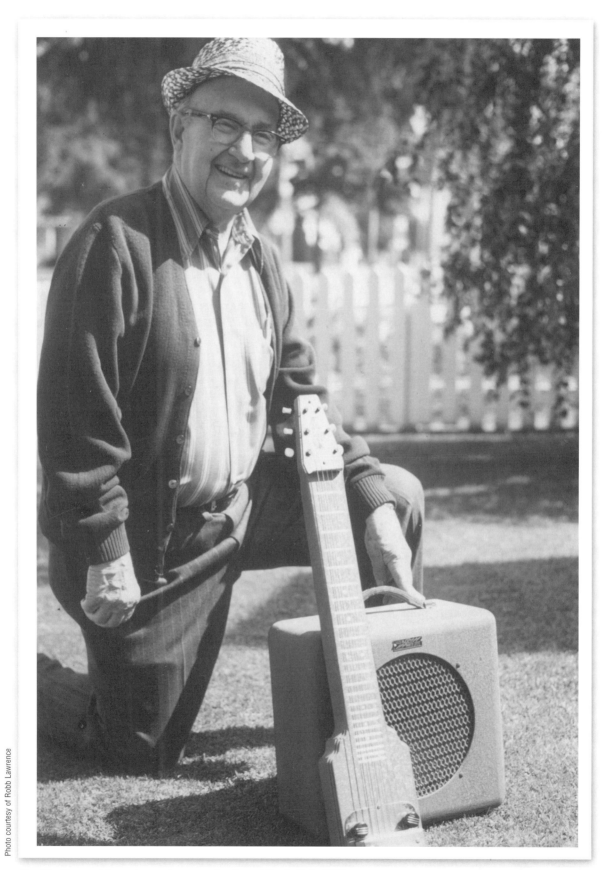

Doc Kauffman with a guitar and amp set that he and Leo built in 1945.

Doc Kauffman working with his father on the farm in Kansas.

Doc Kauffman and his wife Elsie.

*Jim Ford: worked for Leo building
lap steel guitars and amplifiers [in 1945].*

expand the business. He was weary of the future, and memories of his life during the Depression lingered. He feared the guitar business would not last and might cause him to lose everything if the business faltered.

He told Leo, "I think I would rather sell my half of the business to you because I'm afraid of the future." So Leo and Doc dissolved their partnership in January 1946, but remained lifelong friends until Doc's death in 1990.

To learn more about Doc's life, I spent some time with his son, Ken Kauffman. He told me Doc was an only child, born in a log cabin in 1906 in Cedar County, Missouri. During his school years, he spent his spare time working with his father on the farm. Doc described himself as a "real mechanical farmer musician." He always had the feeling he was supposed to do something involving music. He learned to play the piano at an early age and got a piano-playing job at a local theatre for $3 a night.

Later, Doc's interest in the violin prompted him to enroll at Bethany College. He spent two years at Bethany and became very proficient at the violin, playing all of Fritz Kreisler's solos. Doc married his Kansas sweetheart, Elsie Hattie Schmoock in 1922. They moved to California, and he started up the repair shop in Fullerton, where he met Leo.

After Doc left the business, Leo changed the company name to Fender Manufacturing Co. He had several people working in his guitar shop. One was Jim Ford, who had just gotten out of the Navy and was trying to get settled into a civilian life. Jim worked hard building guitars and amplifiers. He started work in late 1945, but shortly after that he wanted to leave to attend UCLA. Even though Leo offered him a chance to manage the shop, Jim left early in 1946 to attend classes at UCLA.

Soon after this, Dale Hyatt came to work for Leo. Dale was made foreman over the guitar and amplifier manufacturing process. Once the buildings were completed at the Pomona Ave. address, Leo moved the manufacturing business to the new location, leaving the radio repair shop and store at the 107 S. Spadra location. (Spadra Road later became Harbor Blvd., which it remains today.)

The new location gave them plenty of room to expand. It was here where Fender grew into a large international manufacturer and a big influence on many styles of music around the world.

Chapter 3
A New Beginning

Leo and I became aquatinted in 1947. It wasn't the radio repair business that drew me to him, but his Ford van with speakers mounted on the outside. Leo used this van to announce special events to people in town. He played music and made announcements as he drove around. I would see this van occasionally, and I wondered who provided this service. So one day, I decided to stop at the radio repair shop, which was responsible for this special and unique way of advertising.

The owner was Leo. We visited awhile, and he told me about his ideas for building some new electronic products. He even asked me if I would like to help him with his advertising mobile unit. I told him I would be willing to work with him.

Leo and I had many things in common. We were both interested in electronics. I studied for a career in electronics and was employed by

Lockheed Aircraft. I also had thoughts of a career in music since I already played guitar in a band every weekend.

Leo seemed interested by my guitar playing. He asked me if I would field-test some of the steel guitars and amplifiers he was building. I told him I didn't know anything about steel guitars, but I would be willing to help any way I could.

I saw Leo many times when I went into his store, which was located in the front part of his repair shop. I went there to get phonograph records or other things I needed. His store was the only place in town to buy phonograph records, sheet music, songbooks, small radios, and other music-related items.

His store was also the first and only place in town that sold television sets. To advertise that product, he mounted a TV in the front window of his store and placed a speaker outside. Just about every night there was a large crowd of people standing outside watching television. Most people did not have television sets in their homes at that time, and this was a way for many people to see the available shows.

Since Leo and I were both interested in electronics, we spent quite a bit of time talking about the subject. On several different occasions, Leo would ask me to take something for testing. This was fine with me because I wanted to learn all I could about electrical circuits.

The two metal buildings where Leo made the lap steel guitars and amplifiers on Pomona Ave. and Santa Fe Ave. The instrument sets had been made previously at the radio shop location.

Around this same time, Leo had just completed construction of two metal buildings and moved his manufacturing facility from the radio repair shop to these new buildings. Every time I saw Leo, he asked me to come to work for him. I told him I was not interested in steel guitars and amplifiers and that I wanted to continue my studies of electronics.

One day Leo called me and said, "Why don't you stop by my new place and see what we are doing?" I told him I would. He proudly showed me his new manufacturing buildings. He asked me again to work for him.

He said, "Why don't you come over and spend a few days to learn about what we are doing and maybe help out a little bit, to better understand this business." I told him I would.

I stayed about three days and did some repair work on several small amplifiers. After that, I told Leo again I was not interested in this work and would not be back.

He said, "Let's go get a cup of coffee and talk about some of the new things that I would like to do."

During our conversation, Leo told me he would like to build a solid-body electric guitar and asked me what I thought about this plan. I told him I thought it would be a great thing to do.

Then he asked me, "Would you be interested working with me on this new project?"

Immediately, I said, "Yes, I would be very interested in something like this."

I started working in his new facility, helping all I could with the building of the steel guitars and amplifiers. In a few weeks, Leo sold his radio repair business to Dale Hyatt, who had been foreman in the guitar-building business. Dale left and started operating the radio repair business.

The foreman's work that Dale had been doing was given to me. Leo and I worked during the day manufacturing steel guitars and amplifiers. After the day's work was over, Leo and I worked on designing a new solid-body electric guitar. We worked every night and on the weekends, sometimes until the wee hours.

Chapter 4
Building the Broadcaster

We started the project to build a solid-body electric guitar in early 1948. It was the beginning of the new Broadcaster guitar.

Those early days were quite difficult. Money was scarce. We had to try everything we could to get this new project off the ground. One of the things we discussed before designing the instrument was how and why we were doing this. Leo and I spent a lot of time making notes on the important qualities we wanted to build into our new type of guitar. Mostly we wanted to solve the problems created by pickups mounted inside hollow-body guitars. One major issue was the horrible feedback the instrument created. Engineers at studios hated this problem.

Another problem was the way hollow-body guitars were built. If a musician's guitar was broken or damaged, it had to be sent back to the factory for repair. This process took a long time and was quite expensive. Most guitar players could only afford one instrument, and if this instrument had to be repaired, the musician was out of work. In those days there were no instrument rental services.

Leo and I thought about these undesirable situations facing guitar players, and this was the basis we used in our designs for a new style of guitar. In addition to having a pickup without the feedback problem, our new guitar had to have a neck that was easy to replace and a lightweight body that was comfortable for the player. The guitar had to be designed so that any part could be replaced in a few minutes, to get the player back in business. It would also have to be easy to build and low-priced.

Leo and I spent many nights in smoky beer joints and clubs talking to guitar players about their ideas or problems. Rather than tell them what we were trying to accomplish, we were mostly interested in what they were telling us. You can learn a lot by listening to people without influencing them.

Leo and I worked many long hours searching for ways to perfect our new project. Many times we'd stay up as late as 2 a.m. Neither of us took time off for anything else. We worked Saturdays, Sundays, and holidays on this project. It required a lot of dedicated effort. We wanted to make sure we were not copying something that someone else had already done. True inventors must rely on the talent and knowledge that God gives them in order to see true results.

After the design plans were complete, we started building several prototypes, which was very challenging. We also had to build our own tooling and dies for the metal parts in our machine shop. In those early days, we went to Los Angeles for all of the material we used to make metal and wood parts for our prototype units.

In particular, electronic parts were hard to find because the war effort consumed everything available. One of the most difficult items to find was the small wire for winding pickups. The size

First prototype electric solid-body guitar built by Leo Fender and George Fullerton in 1948. This instrument started the "Fabulous" Fender guitar company.

we needed was #42 plain enameled wire, which was specially coated for insulation between each layer of wire on the pickup.

There was a large wire company in Huntington Park that made this size and kind of wire, but the defense work had taken everything it made. This company had a large warehouse where all of the older material and mostly scrap wire was stored. The only source for getting this special wire was to search through the partially used rolls and others that were not acceptable to sell.

If we took enough time and carefully looked through the stacks of dusty material, we could usually find a small amount of wire needed to wind the pickups for our testing purposes. Sometimes I would spend a whole day searching through this discarded wire.

We tested the best kind of wood to use for making the bodies and necks. We wanted to use pine for the bodies because it was lightweight, good quality, and easy to get. The pine we used then was of a very high quality compared with the pine available today.

We tried many ways to make the pine suitable for bodies, but it was so soft that it dented easily, which made the bodies look bad. We even built a vacuum tank to hold two bodies submerged in a special sealing liquid. We pulled a strong vacuum to draw out the air from the bodies, and the sealing solution was completely absorbed through the

wood. We were hoping this would seal all the wood fibers together. However, this did not solve the problem of the wood being too soft. (Several of the pine-body prototypes are still around today. They are valuable to guitar collectors and fetch a handsome price.) After testing several kinds of wood for the bodies, we chose lightweight ash. This was a fairly stable wood and had a good-looking grain that was easy to finish.

The necks on these prototypes were made out of hard rock maple and did not have truss rods. We had hoped the necks would be strong enough without truss rods, but they were not stable enough. The string pressure caused them to bow. Therefore we had to install truss rods in the necks. After we designed a way to do this, they worked perfectly.

We then started the production line work. Some of the ash lumber was quite wide. In order to use this wide lumber, we made a saw cut in the center and then glued the pieces back together to prevent the wood from cupping.

After this, the wood blanks were ready for the routing and machining work. The edges of the body were shaped with a radius all around the outside, except for the opening, where the neck would be attached later in assembly. The bodies were completely hand sanded to a very smooth condition. After an inspection, they were passed on to the finishing department.

My father, Fred Fullerton, working on bandsaw in the Fender woodshop on Pomona Ave.

After much hard work and dedication, this new guitar was introduced to the public one night when Leo and I took it to the Riverside Rancho, a club in Los Angeles. This was a popular ballroom where different bands played. We went there hoping that we would get the guitar players to try out our new instrument.

While we waited over in one corner for the band to take a break, a young man saw us and came over and asked what kind of instrument we had.

He asked, "Can I try it?"

We told him that was why we were there, to get someone to try out this new style of guitar.

When the band took a break, he asked the leader of the group if he could plug this guitar into one of their amplifiers.

He said, "Sure, go ahead."

This young man sat on the edge of the stage and played this guitar for about two hours. The band members and the dancers crowded around and watched and listened in complete amazement and admiration for the wonderful exhibition of guitar playing by this young man. The band never went back on. And the dancers never moved away from this extraordinary demonstration of something brand new.

The young man was the famous Jimmy Bryant. And after Jimmy started using the new guitar, everyone wanted a guitar like his. Our manufacturing facility could not produce enough instruments to meet the demand. This prompted us to get busy and expand our working space, to try to keep up with the large number of guitars being ordered.

Photo courtesy of Robb Lawrence

The Broadcaster guitar.

This newly designed electric guitar become famous in 1950. We called it the Broadcaster. But we had to change the name soon afterward because another company was already using the name.

During the process of changing names, the guitars bore only the Fender name on the headstock. We cut off the word "Broadcaster" from the decals. We did this in order to keep production going until the new decals were available. (These instruments are called Nocasters by vintage guitar people.)

Eventually, we selected the name Telecaster. Our naming process was influenced by technology of the time. The radio was the greatest means of hearing music in the early days. Therefore, Broadcaster was used to show the importance of how such an instrument could be used for radio broadcasting. When the name change became necessary, television was making its mark on the airwaves. So the name Telecaster was an appropriate choice.

We also built another guitar during this time. It was as good as the others, but it had only one pickup, which was mounted in the bridge plate.

23

Top view of Telecaster.

Back view of Telecaster, hand-signed by George Fullerton.

David Smith with his never-been-played 1951 Telecaster Guitar, serial #0900. This guitar was a wedding present to Gene Smith, David's father, from George Fullerton in 1952.

This concrete-block building was erected in 1950 in order to expand the work space for building guitars and amps.

We called this guitar Esquire, using the distinguished title of a country gentleman. The control plate looked the same on all three instruments, with two control knobs and a three-position lever switch, but the wiring diagram was different on the Esquire.

The year 1950 was a busy and rewarding time for the company. One of the great accomplishments was the addition of a concrete block building on the property on Pomona Ave. This new facility added a great deal of working space and allowed us to produce more new instruments.

Chapter 5
Creating the Precision Bass

Since the Telecaster was such a tremendous success, Leo and I were encouraged to move on to other new products. One of the specialty items Leo wanted as a high priority was a solid-body electric bass. There was no instrument of this kind available, except for the big upright bass. It was the perfect time to work on some designs for another completely new kind of instrument.

The challenge of designing an electric bass seemed beyond imagination. Since there was nothing available as far as parts go to produce this new instrument, we realized that we would have to make everything from scratch. Leo wanted to design a bass in the same style as the Telecaster guitar and wanted it to have frets on the fingerboard.

One of the greatest challenges in designing the prototype was finding strings that worked with an electric pickup. The only strings available at the time were so-called "catgut" strings for the upright acoustic bass, which could not pick up the magnetic signal. We contacted several string manufacturers,

Photo by Leo Fender

One of the first-built Precision bass instruments, 1952.

but none of them had anything that would work. We tried every size of string available, as well as many different kinds and sizes of wire, but none were acceptable. We had just about reached the end of the road for the electric bass, when in desperation, we tried something different.

Using a set of catgut strings, we tightly wrapped and glued some fine-gauge steel wire around the part of the string where it passed over the magnetic pole. This was the magic that gave us the first working model of the solid-body electric bass.

When we had a working prototype, we started a testing process. We wanted to find out how well this new item would be accepted by working musicians. The acceptance for the instrument was overwhelming. This gave us the encouragement to go ahead and make the tooling so we could produce these basses.

For the first time, the bass player could now be heard by everyone in the clubs and dance halls, just like players of the electric guitar. Not only could he be heard quite clearly, it offered him

another big advantage: the new bass was easier to transport. Previously, he had to haul his bass on the top of a car or inside a station wagon.

However, we faced another problem immediately. What kind of an amplifier could handle the low bass tones and supply the volume needed?

We started working on amplifier designs to serve this purpose. We soon learned that the loudspeakers available were not heavy enough for this project. But with the help of samples from speaker companies, we made a test amplifier that sounded good. We used heavy 15-inch speakers that handled the deep bass notes. The amplifier had a bottom-mounted chassis, but the controls were mounted in the top of the cabinet. This was the first amplifier built specially for basses. We named it Bassman.

The new Precision bass and the Bassman amplifier were introduced in 1951 and became an instant success. The new electric bass and amplifier were the talk of the town. They were the newest equipment for bass playing and added

Photo courtesy of Robb Lawrence

*1952 Precision bass with a
1953 Bassman amplifier. (PG)*

dimension to the musician's technique. The bass
and amplifier were strictly Leo's babies. They
were his idea completely. That's why he is known
around the world as the "Father of the Electric
Bass." I am thankful to have had a part in helping
him fulfill his dream.

Chapter 6
Developing the Stratocaster Guitar

After the Precision bass and Bassman amplifiers were put into production, we started thinking about another guitar to give the players something the Telecaster guitar did not offer.

We had received many requests for a guitar with vibrato. Some players had seen a guitar with vibrato designed and built by Paul Bigsby, and they were interested in seeing what we might develop.

In early 1952, we started working on ideas for this brand-new instrument. In order to design something different, we sought information from the players. After a lot of inquiries in the field, we were able to make a list of desired features.

The name selected for this new instrument was Stratocaster, mainly because it was a higher level of sound and different than anything else on the market. The first shipment was made in September 1954. The Stratocaster guitar became a sensational new invention. The intense interest and desire for this new guitar created a startling wave of excitement.

The Stratocaster helped make Fender instruments a part of the dress code for many bands and

Photo courtesy of Robb Lawrence

A 1955 Sunburst Stratocaster guitar. (PG)

entertainers all around the world. But people have questioned our success. Articles were written that Fender was about to go into bankruptcy in 1954. They were false. The true position of company was strong.

We had many products in production and could hardly fill the orders that we received. We were hiring people all the time to help produce more products. At the same time, we had completed three new buildings and were starting on more new buildings. This was a carefully controlled operating organization, and we were quite successful.

It's gratifying to note that the first three solid-body electric instruments that Leo and I designed and produced, namely the Telecaster guitar, the Precision bass, and the Stratocaster guitar, have been the leaders and most desired electric instruments in the world for 50 years. This is a fantastic record by any standard.

These three buildings comprised the Fender factory until it was moved to S. Raymond Ave. in 1953.

The nine original Fender buildings at 500 S. Raymond Ave. in the 1950s.

The same buildings as they appeared in 2002.

Over the years these three instruments have become true musical icons in the electric instrument world. They are the instruments that became the base structure for the Fender Electric Instrument Co. Many people have copied these instruments. Some of the copies may look good, but they are still just copies.

Chapter 7

The Jazzmaster and Color Bursts on the Scene

Jazz musicians asked Leo and me many times if we planned to build electric guitars and basses for their use. So in 1957, we started designing a new jazz guitar. There were many things that had to be explored regarding the sound, function, and appearance of a completely new type of guitar. A key employee, Freddie Tavares, was a big help in this design. Because Freddie was a working musician, he knew what jazz musicians wanted. In 1958, the Jazzmaster, with its offset-waist design and the pre-set control system, was introduced.

The Jazzmaster was also significant because it launched the company into offering colored instruments. It all started when I kept one of the 1957 Jazzmaster prototypes to do some experimenting with color. At this time, our line did not include colored instruments. However, we had made colored instruments for players by special order. I felt we should offer a choice of color.

George Fullerton playing a 1957 Prototype Jazzmaster guitar. The color is "Fullerton Red." (PG)

One day I went to a local paint store and told the man in charge, "I would like to have a special color mixed." I really didn't know what color I was looking for, except that it should be some shade of red.

He and I went into his back room where he had hundreds of different shades of all colors. But after looking through these samples, I didn't see any like what I had in mind.

The man mixed several different samples, until finally I picked out a certain color that was like what I sought. He mixed a can of paint for me to try out on a guitar body.

The prototype Jazzmaster guitar was dismantled

and the raw-wood body was used to test the color. A light-colored undercoat was sprayed on the body and then lightly sanded. Next, the special red color was sprayed on the body. After drying, another coat of red was applied. After this dried, the finish was sanded with 500-grit sandpaper, and the body was polished to a high sheen. After being polished, the red color seemed to glow. The light-colored undercoats were the reason the red looked so special. The workers in the factory referred to this as "Fullerton Red," since the paint did not have its own name.

When the red prototype guitar was completed, it was sent to the sales office to get the salespeople's reactions. They got a big laugh from this. They said, "Who would want a red guitar?" And they sent it back with a very negative report on its appearance.

This discouraged me, but I continued to believe that there must be some color that would appeal to musicians. Finally, I got the company to allow a few of these red guitars to be built and sent into the field. When this happened—to everyone's surprise and disbelief—they were well accepted by musicians who were excited to play the red guitars.

The sales company ordered only a small number of the red guitars at first, and immediately sold every one. This prompted them to pursue the color a bit further.

In order to get enough red lacquer to complete a run of these instruments, we had to get our regular paint supplier to mix it for us. When the supplier sent the new red lacquer to us, it was called "Fiesta Red." It was amazing how fast Fiesta Red became one of the most desired guitar colors.

After the incredible acceptance of Fiesta Red for instruments, the company started experimenting with other colors. We relied on Duco colors, which were basically automotive colors. These paints could be purchased almost anywhere, so the customer could easily touch up or completely refinish the instrument.

These were some of the colors eventually selected:

Dakota Red

Candy Apple Red - metallic

Lake Placid Blue - metallic

Sonic Blue

Daphne Blue

Fire Mist Gold - metallic

Shoreline Gold - metallic

Inca Sliver - metallic

Charcoal Mist Frost - metallic

Olympic White

Black

Teal Green - metallic

Foam Green

Shell Pink

The original 1957 Jazzmaster guitar with the special Fiesta Red color is still in my collection. I will always cherish this instrument. It meant a great deal to have had a big part introducing color to our guitars.

Chapter 8
Innovation Continues

Over the years, several new guitars, basses, and amplifiers were added to the Fender line. The list of new models included Musicmaster guitars, available with a short- and long-scale string length; Duo-Sonic guitars, with short and long string length; Mustang guitars, with vibrato; and also Mustang basses.

We added a pedal steel guitar, with one or two eight-string necks, and a four-string electric mandolin. There was also an electric violin, and two models of foot pedals, as well as various-

Two Fender violins in a case.

sized amplifiers. The company also purchased the Rhodes Electric Piano Co.

In 1960, the company designed and produced the Jazz bass. This bass was quite different than the Precision bass. It was designed to attract jazz players in need of an electric instrument.

The body shape was similar to the Jazzmaster guitar, with an offset-waist design. The instrument had two pickups that covered a wider range of tone than the Precision bass. It featured a sunburst finish, which was applied the same way as the sunburst on a Stratocaster guitar. It was also available in a variety of colors. The Jazz bass was a good item for many years, but it was never as popular as the Precision bass.

In 1960, Roger Rossmeisl came to the factory to see Leo. He was interested in building acoustic guitars for Fender. Roger's knowledge and experience with acoustics came from his father and his German background. Leo always wanted to have a line of acoustic instruments, but we did not have anyone in the company who could do this type of work. Leo was impressed with the guitars that Roger brought to the factory. Leo and Roger came to an agreement, and Roger started designing a line of acoustic guitars for us.

To do this right, we needed a completely different building so Roger would have the necessary equipment and space to begin making these additional products. Roger worked quickly, and before long he had all of the equipment needed for this project. In a short time, he introduced the new model acoustic guitars. He designed and built several different kinds and sizes of instruments.

The flattop, six-string models were named Kingman, Palamino, Malibu, and Newporter. The Shenandoah was a twelve-string model. The special arched-top guitars were constructed from the finest material available. Every part was hand-made and of excellent quality. They were called "LTD" models. Records show only 36 of these were made. Some of them can be seen occasionally at guitar shows.

In 1961, the company introduced the Jaguar guitar. It had the same cutaway body, with the offset-waist design of the Jazzmaster, but the components were different.

The innovation and quality in Fender products is indisputable. There were many people responsible for this. Some, in fact, left their mark on their work. Occasionally, players have found names written on the inside of their instruments and on the butt-end of the necks. The names have special importance. Many people rely on these names as an identifying mark of a genuine pre-CBS Fender instrument. The vintage guitars with names are most desired.

Here are two names that appear on the instruments:

Gloria—Gloria Fuentes worked for Fender for many years and was considered one of its most valuable employees. Her name is written on the inside of hundreds of instruments. Over the years, the presence of "Gloria" has come to symbolize the highest degree of quality. She became disappointed when CBS bought the company and started cutting the quality of the product. She did not remain long after the company was sold.

Tadeo Gomez:
The name "Tadeo" is written on the butt-end of hundreds of guitar necks. Tadeo did the final sanding of the necks. Necks featuring his name are considered to be better products, and established them as genuine pre-CBS instruments. He worked until CBS bought the company and then retired.

Tadeo—Tadeo Gomez was a trusted and dependable employee for many years. He wrote his name on the backside of the butt-ends of hundreds of guitar necks. Tadeo did the final sanding of the necks before they were sent to the finishing department. He was good at making the necks have a perfectly smooth feel and fine shape. He retired around the time CBS bought the company.

George Fullerton playing a 1957 prototype Jazzmaster guitar.
The color is "Fullerton Red."

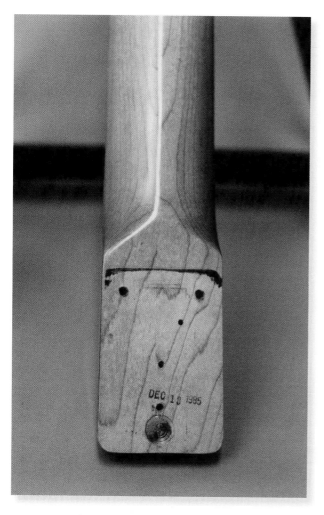

Broadcaster neck, dated 12-13-85.

Broadcaster guitar.

Neck socket of Broadcaster guitar, inspected and signed by Leo Fender, 1-2-86.

(Photos courtesy of Tim Page.)

1984 SB-2 bass.
(Photo courtesy of Tim Page.)

1981 fretless L-2000 bass.
(Photo courtesy of Tim Page.)

G&L instrument color chart.

ASAT bass in blonde with gun-oil tint neck.

(Photo courtesy of David McLaren.)

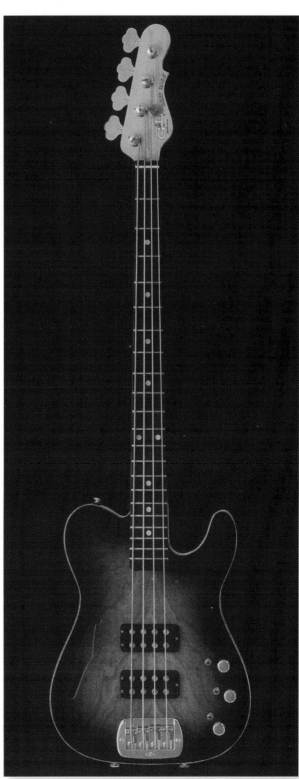

ASAT semi-hollow bass in 3-tone sunburst with wood binding.

(Photo courtesy of David McLaren.)

Rare 1986 SC-3 guitar with gold hardware
and without pickguard.

(Photos courtesy of Tim Page.)

1989 black SC-3 guitar with pickguard
signed by George Fullerton.

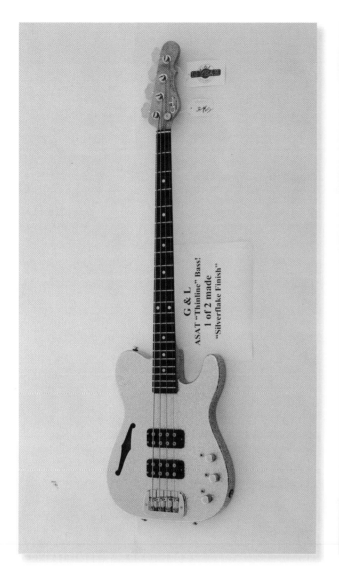

First prototype of semi-hollow ASAT bass
in silverflake finish.

1991 ASAT bass in cherryburst finish,
without "Leo Fender" decal.

1990 ASAT Classic in 3-tone sunburst with "Leo Fender" decal.

(Photos courtesy of Tim Page.)

Mural on the north side of a parking structure
on the site of the original Fender factory.

Mural on the south side.

Rare ASAT III with MFD bridge humbucker.
(Photo courtesy of Jeff Byrd and Tim Page.)

Blonde 1986 ASAT guitar with two single-coil pickups.
(Photo courtesy of Jeff Byrd and Tim Page.)

G&L 20th-anniversary model; 1 of 50.
2-tone sunburst with bird's eye maple neck
finished with gun-oil tint.

Neck plate of 20th-anniversary model; 1 of 50.

Limited-edition ASAT JR. Trans-red finish on body and neck.

(Photos courtesy of Tim Page.)

Legacy Special with dual-blade pickups.

ASAT S-3 left-handed in red swirl red finish (discontinued).

ASAT Special in goldflake with gun-oil tinted neck.

(Photos courtesy of Tim Page.)

Fretless L-2500 5-string bass in 3-tone sunburst.

(Photo courtesy of David McLaren.)

JB-2 bass in honeyburst over flame mapletop.

(Photo courtesy of David McLaren.)

Chapter 9

CBS Buys Fender, Sells Fender

Fender continued operating in a highly successful manner until 1965 when CBS bought the company and put it under the control of the Columbia records division.

One of the main reasons Leo sold was because his health seemed to be failing, and he did not want to pass along the leadership to someone else. Leo wanted to remain in the top position in the company as long as he was able to carry out the necessary responsibilities.

As a condition of the sale, Leo signed a five-year agreement in which he agreed not to do anything that would compete against CBS.

After CBS took control of the company in early 1965, changes in the operation happened quickly. Many valuable employees who had been with the company a long time were laid off. In particular, it seemed people who lacked a formal education and college degree were vulnerable to dismissal. The changes in personnel and in the production methods caused the quality of the products to suffer.

Leo was not pleased about the changes. He became unhappy having an office in the factory and wanted to be in a more neutral place. He rented a small

Photo courtesy of Robb Lawrence

Bill Schultz:
CEO and Chairman of the Board of the Fender Company. Bill was asked about the future prospects of the company. He said, "Building on the Fender legacy, the current Fender organization has developed to a financially sound company and a leader in creating and technology."

building for his office and workshop. This building was located several blocks from the factory. There he was able to do the things that pleased him most.

Between 1965 and 1970, almost all of the leadership and most of the engineering and design people were replaced. The turmoil caused quite a few people to resign and move to companies where they were more appreciated.

After spending five years with CBS Fender, I felt my time was being wasted on unproductive tasks. I became disenchanted with the way the company treated me. They lowered my salary and changed my position several times in just a few months. The changes were unsettling and made me and others feel part of an unstable operation.

The new Fender factory facility in Corona, CA, completed in September 1998.

George Fullerton signing a guitar for Fred Stuart—a master builder at the Fender Custom Shop.

After carefully thinking about my future, I decided to resign in March 1970. I had spent more than 20 years with the Fender organization, and I felt it was time to make a change. I left the company in good standing. They gave me full separation pay for my years of service, as well as many other benefits. Even after leaving the company, I felt that sooner or later I would get back in the music business.

There was a great lull in the effectiveness of the company; it seemed to be just barely afloat. Something had to be done, so CBS officials decided the best way out was to offer the company for sale.

The president of CBS Fender at the time, Bill Schultz, put a group together to buy the company. Bill had been president for a while and had many years of experience at other companies. And on March 12, 1985, Bill and his capable team took over the weakened Fender and moved it to Corona, Calif. Bill remains Fender's chief executive officer and chairman of the board today.

Bill began the difficult process of building the company back to its original stature. Little by lit-

John Page: he started the Fender Custom Shop.

tle, the company recovered Fender's good name and recaptured the quality in the original products.

One of the more recent, valuable innovations at Fender is its Custom Shop. John Page, who

John English: a master builder at the Fender Custom Shop.

Fred Stuart: a master builder at the Fender Custom Shop.

worked in Fender research and development, dreamed of having a large operation dedicated to building custom instruments. He and Michael Stevens made the shop a reality. It makes the standard Telecaster and Stratocaster guitars and Precision bass into specialty items. My son, Geoff Fullerton, is part of this customizing operation. He is the third generation of Fullertons to be part of Fender. I'm proud to have him follow me in the instrument-building business.

Yasuhiko and Miyoko Iwanade: Yasuhiko is a former employee of the Fender Custom Shop.

Also recently, Fender created the Museum of the Arts Foundation to commemorate and celebrate musical achievements. Soon after the foundation was established, John left the Custom Shop to become its executive director.

Fender Custom Shop Instruments

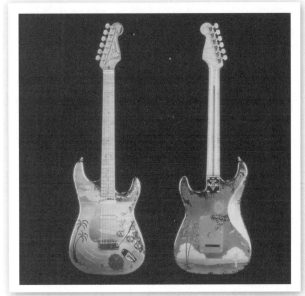

(PG)

Fender Custom Shop Instruments

(PG)

(PG)

(PG)

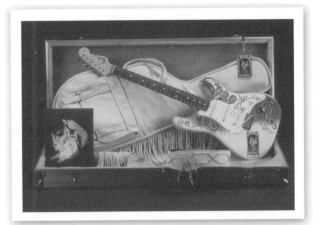

Ray Winchel, his wife Mary, and daughter Bonnie.
They live in Scottsdale, AZ where he is Assistant Manager
of the Fender order credit dept.

Bill and Susan Carson. They have been an important team
for the Fender company. They worked together managing
a large sales territory in the Nashville, TN area.

Chapter 10
Leo's Life After Fender

When Leo left Fender, he experienced freedoms that he never had before. To that point, his life had been spent immersed in work. He now realized he could take time to travel anywhere he wanted to go.

He and his wife Esther began taking car trips to many historical and scenic places across the United States. They also traveled to Hawaii and Alaska several times. After these shorter domestic trips, they branched out by taking cruises to other countries.

While they preferred to cruise, they wanted to visit the Holy Land, but had to go by plane. After visiting many of the famous sites in Israel, they decided to go to Egypt. They were told the best way to travel to Egypt was by train.

Leo's train trip to Egypt remains one of the most vivid travel tales he ever told. It was quite a long distance to travel and part of it passed through some hot desert areas. The only people who lived and traveled in the desert were Bedouins and Nomadic tribes who moved about constantly in search of food and pasture for their animals.

Leo and Esther Fender. Esther was Leo's first wife. This picture was taken in Egypt near the great Pyramids.

These people traveled along the railroad tracks because they were smoother than the rough desert floor and a better place for their animals to walk. Because of this, large amounts of animal droppings settled in the dust along the tracks. As the train passed over, it whipped up large swirls of this foul-smelling mixture. Since the trains were not tightly sealed, a lot of this smelly dust entered the cars.

Leo and Esther nearly suffocated from the heat and dust that seeped in through the cracks. They were happy and relieved to have this trip end. They wanted some relief from all this discomfort.

Leo said, "I will never travel by train again in this arid world. I will never encourage anyone else to travel by train in this part of the world."

Even though getting to Egypt was painful, they visited many places of historic value while there, including the Valley of the Kings, where many of the great pharaohs are buried. They traveled down the Nile River to the city of Aswan and its great Aswan High Dam. They also went on a camel ride near the great Pyramids of Giza. They enjoyed this very much.

The Egypt trip made Leo crave more time at home. He started an operation called CLF Research Corp., which stood for Clarence Leo Fender. He used it for all sorts of personal business. For example, his boat, Aqua Fen, was registered through CLF. He also bought some property under CLF and constructed a series of commercial buildings for income on one of the plots. He had to pay for the street on the side of the property, which began at Placentia Ave. and ended at State College Blvd. Somehow he got the city of Fullerton to let him name it Fender Ave. The commercial buildings housed many businesses, each with a front office and warehouse space. He was beginning to think about the guitar industry again and even reserved two of the buildings to use as facilities to build musical instruments.

Tom Walker and Forrest White kicked Leo's thinking into high gear when they contacted him about adding stringed instruments to their line of amplifiers. Leo, Tom, and Forrest already had a history together. Leo had loaned them the money to start Musitek, which was later renamed Tri-Sonix. They also renamed the company again, at Leo's suggestion. Leo created the name MusicMan, saying it was better for working with dealers and more acceptable to musicians.

Regardless of what they called the company, Tom and Forrest knew they needed electric guitars and basses to offer a complete line of products to music retailers. They also asked if I would be interested in working with Leo to design and build a line of instruments. I said, "Yes, I would be very interested in taking part in that venture."

After working on the initial details, Leo and I decided we didn't want to work directly for MusicMan, but would build our own factory and manufacture instruments to sell to MusicMan. Leo suggested we work under CLF Research Corp., so he transferred his personal property and other financial interests out of CLF. We agreed to work as partners. I owned 34% of the factory, and he owned 66%.

Tom was an amplifier designer, but Forrest didn't have any experience in design. That's why they asked Leo and I to design the instruments from scratch. Forrest did have a headstock design he thought was great. He told us we should get a design patent on it. But Leo told Forrest that a design ought to be something that someone would want to steal. That tells you what Leo thought of Forrest's design.

We used our experience designing the Fender instruments as the foundation on which to take guitar and bass designs to the next level. We used some basic elements from the successful Fender instruments and added new features to improve sound and versatility. By the '70s, music had changed, and we wanted to build instruments to satisfy musicians' demands. Just like we did in the '50s, we talked to a lot of guitarists and bassists about what they wanted in their instruments. We did field research continuously—not just when designing a new model. We wanted to make sure our instruments kept getting better.

Back in the '50s, basses were rhythm instruments. But by the '70s, bassists were also using them as lead instruments. By the '70s, rock music had a big, fat, distorted guitar sound, and we wanted to design a guitar that would give this to the musicians but in an instrument that was comfortable, easy to play, and easy to repair. So we took the best elements of our Fender designs and evolved them to suit the modern music.

Chapter 11

The Founding of CLF Research Corp. and MusicMan

Building instruments for MusicMan seemed full of good possibilities. So we set up a working area in one of the new buildings on E. Fender Ave. We were working as CLF Research Corp; again, the new operation for designing and manufacturing electric instruments was owned completely by Leo and I, not MusicMan.

I started work on Dec. 1, 1974. At that time I was working alone. Leo had not yet moved his office and workshop into the building.

Leo hired a man named Ronnie Beers when he was constructing the new buildings. Ronnie was a skilled metal worker and welder and would be valuable in this new venture. Very soon he and Leo moved into the new building.

We had a big job ahead of us in designing and proving the feasibility of the first model. We had plans to design a full line of fine electric guitars and basses. All that had to be done before equipping the manufacturing facility.

MusicMan Stingray guitar.

MusicMan Stingray bass.

Since we had gone through this process when we started Fender, we thought it would be much easier. It wasn't. The days were long and tiring, but we were making progress toward a new goal. In order to build instruments, we had to have the necessary equipment to do the job right. The work really got started in 1975.

We had to design and build much of the new machinery and equipment because there was nothing available that was suitable for the work we planned to do. There was a long list of things needed before production at the factory could

start. Putting together a guitar factory from the ground up is tough; the time and money that must go into a project of this size is incredible. Our experience with Fender proved to be one of our most valuable assets, but costs were still mounting each day.

It took a lot of money, time, and effort to both design the instruments and create the factory in which to build them. For every part of the guitar, we had to design the part itself, make drawings for the tool-and-die maker, work with the maker so the die was correct, order metal, then make

MusicMan guitar prototype number 2, built in 1976. This instrument is property of Johnny McLaren.

Backside of the MusicMan guitar prototype number 2, built in 1976.

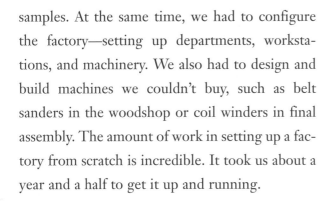

samples. At the same time, we had to configure the factory—setting up departments, workstations, and machinery. We also had to design and build machines we couldn't buy, such as belt sanders in the woodshop or coil winders in final assembly. The amount of work in setting up a factory from scratch is incredible. It took us about a year and a half to get it up and running.

One of the most delicate tools needed was a coil winding mechanism for winding pickups. This had to be built in a specific way in order to properly wind the pickup coils, and required a fair amount of ingenuity in its design.

Leo and I always preferred hand-wound pickups for the instruments we built, because we felt machine-

This shows the MusicMan name, prototype number, and date: January 1976.

MusicMan bass prototype number 3, dated February 1976. This instrument is the property of Johnny McLaren.

Back of the MusicMan bass prototype number 3, dated February 1976.

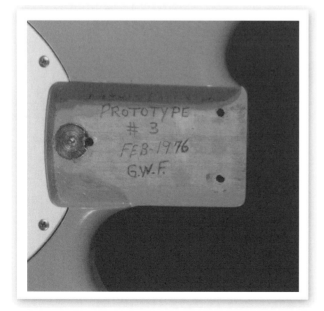

This shows the neck socket of the MusicMan bass prototype number 3, dated February 1976.

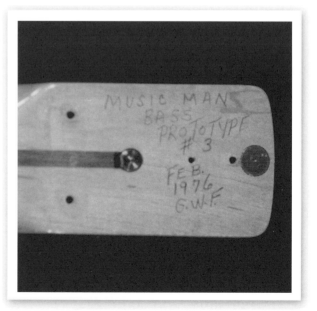

The butt-end of the neck on the MusicMan bass prototype number 3, dated February 1976.

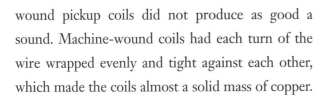

MusicMan bass prototype number 1, dated December 1975. This instrument is the property of Johnny McLaren.

Backside of the MusicMan bass prototype number 1, dated December 1975.

wound pickup coils did not produce as good a sound. Machine-wound coils had each turn of the wire wrapped evenly and tight against each other, which made the coils almost a solid mass of copper.

The coils that were wound on a hand-controlled winder were quite uneven. The crisscrossing of different turns left many small open spaces between each turn, which allowed the magnetic field to saturate the coil more fully.

By winding the coil unevenly, we changed the capacitance, which helped the stored electrical charge to operate more efficiently. It just naturally seemed like a better way to wind pickup coils. There was just one question. How would this be possible on a large scale?

Designing and building a winding mechanism required much trial and error. We tried direct drive, belt drive, gear drive and several other ways, but none seemed to work right. These methods did not have the proper tensioning means of winding the coil. However, we eventually came up with a rather ingenious device.

In winding an oblong-shaped part, such as a pickup coil, the fine copper wire was naturally wound tight over the ends, but the tension dropped, leaving the copper wire loose on the sides as the form completed a turn.

The way we learned to manage this problem was to drive the winder with a sewing machine motor and foot pedal control. We used a small pulley on

The neck socket shows the MusicMan bass prototype number 1, dated December 1975.

This shows the bridge and pickup location on the MusicMan bass prototype number 1, dated December 1975.

the motor shaft and another small pulley on the mandrel that held the coil form.

Simple as it may seem, we used rubber bands to turn these pulleys. The stretching of the rubber bands pulled the copper wire tight over the ends of the form as it was turned. Their reciprocal action kept the tension the same on the sides as on the end.

The problem was solved inexpensively and efficiently. Since this worked so well, another rubber band was used to operate the driver on the turn counter.

The operator of the winder held the fine copper wire delicately between the finger and thumb, as he or she skillfully guided the wire onto the coil form. This procedure required a certain amount of patience and training for the operator to become proficient. When it was done properly, it was a great way to wind pickup coils.

Some people thought all we had to do was copy what we did before and start putting instruments together, but that was not how we wanted to operate our factory. We wanted to build something unique and produce a better product, and that takes a lot of time, effort, and money. This process separates the professionals from the amateurs. After years of designing and building many superb musical instruments, Leo and I agreed that we finally had the way to do it right.

After many months of working on prototype instruments and getting the factory prepared, we were ready. We kept another air compressor, strictly as a standby unit in case of failure in the other equipment. Again experience taught us to be prepared. And on Wednesday, June 23, 1976, we shipped our first instruments to MusicMan. They included seven Stingray I guitars, with serial numbers G001000 through G001006, and seven Stingray basses, with serial numbers

B001000 through B001006. They were to be displayed at that summer's NAMM Show, which was held in Chicago at that time.

Sales of MusicMan instruments grew steadily for the next several months. By the late '70s, MusicMan was successful, but Tom wasn't happy with the arrangement. He wanted MusicMan to build the instruments instead of CLF Research. We offered to teach MusicMan employees how to build instruments at our factory. When they could handle it, we would sell them the tooling, dies, and material. Tom said, "What we really want to do is buy the company you already have and operate it ourselves." But we told him we didn't want to sell. We had invested so much money and effort, and wanted to remain in the guitar-building business. Tom thought I prevented the sale, but Leo didn't want to sell either. Tom seemed to focus on me, getting angry because I would not agree.

After repeated attempts to get us to sell the company, MusicMan began sending smaller and smaller orders for instruments. Regardless of how we tried to negotiate, orders continued to decline. This obviously caused us a problem because our overhead was high. We were not filling enough orders to continue the same way.

At the beginning of the slowdown, we were producing about 60 instruments a day. That number decreased in a short time. Leo and I were quite concerned because we had very little output from the factory, but no decrease in expenses.

Tom and Forrest never made an offer for CLF Research. I think they figured they could somehow get control of CLF without paying for it. Up until then, they had been pretty successful at getting money from Leo without paying it back. Tom and Forrest tried to force us to bow down to their underhanded ways by cutting back orders for instruments. They must have thought this would pressure us into their lowly scheme, but it didn't work. We contacted our attorney and told him what was happening. Tom said there was a written agreement between MusicMan and CLF, stating that CLF would only build instruments for MusicMan. I asked Tom to show me the agreement. He said, "You'll see it in court." There was no written agreement and nothing about building instruments exclusively for MusicMan.

By this point, we had to lay off most employees because MusicMan's orders had stopped. We eventually had to let all of our employees go, except our foreman Lloyd Chewning.

We were in quite a quandary about how to handle the situation. After getting legal advice, we decided that since MusicMan had put us in such a tight situation, we would make changes on our own. We decided to do away with CLF Research Corp. completely. This move infuriated the people at MusicMan. The last thing Tom said to us was that he would make sure we never sold any of our instruments.

We started the new company, G&L Musical Products Inc., and began designing instruments to be sold under the brand name G&L. The "G" stands for George and the "L" for Leo. This was the only name Leo wanted for the company. And the story continues.

PART II

Building G&L and the G&L Way

Chapter 12

G&L Musical Products Inc. Comes on the Scene

When Leo and I started G&L Musical Products, our goal was to build the finest electric instruments in the world. Our many years of experience in designing and building electric instruments gave us a solid base for implementing every phase needed to realize our dream.

Our only employee was our foreman, Lloyd, who had been with us in the Fender days as well as the MusicMan period. Lloyd was helpful in getting prototype instruments built. He was familiar with the equipment and was able to make parts needed for testing. It took us a few months to begin production again, and fortunately, several of our previous employees were eager to come back to work.

In early 1979, we created our first prototype G&L guitar, the F-100 model. The F-100 model with built-in preamplifier was introduced in 1980. We also introduced three models of bass instruments in 1980—the L-1000 bass, L-2000 bass and the L-2000E bass with built-in preamplifier.

Now that the factory was operating again, we needed an outlet for our products. In June 1980, we established our own sales office, G&L Music Sales Inc., and Dale Hyatt came to work the company. Leo was president of the sales company, I was vice president, and Dale was vice president and sales manager. Having Dale aboard seemed like a good move since he had spent many years working in sales at Fender and other companies in the music industry.

MusicMan hung on for a while by selling amplifiers. But the company continued to lose business without musical instruments to complete its line of merchandise. MusicMan closed its doors in October 1983. This was a sad day because it had distributed many fine instruments that Leo and I built. I still see many of these early MusicMan instruments at vintage guitar shows. They are quite sought after and fetch a high price.

We were treated unfairly by MusicMan. The episode caused us a lot of grief and cost us a great deal of money. To this day, I don't know why the MusicMan people pressured us to sell to them. Had they continued as originally planned and allowed CLF Research to grow, MusicMan could have been a world leader in the music industry today.

I don't understand why MusicMan didn't do everything possible to keep itself going strong. Leo and I worked hard designing instruments and building a factory to manufacture them, and were disappointed because the instruments were not being built.

Even though we may have seemed to be the losers in that endeavor, we were given a great opportunity. We were able to use all of our facilities at the well-equipped factory we had built. Our trained personnel were ready and waiting to implement our new designs for instruments. This launched G&L into one of the best American-built instrument companies in the world.

The G&L Factory located at 2548 East Fender Ave., Fullerton, California.

George Fullerton

Leo Fender

Chapter 13

G&L Takes Hold, Leo Lets Go

After we started designing instruments at CLF Research for MusicMan, Leo and Esther still went on a few trips. But soon Esther became ill and was not able to travel. During the MusicMan years and the beginning days of G&L, Esther's health deteriorated. She passed away on August 1, 1979.

Leo was devastated by the death of his wife. His many friends, as well as the people at the factory, helped him through his grief. But it was a sad time for Leo because he didn't have any family and he lived alone.

Seeing G&L grow and watching retailers and players embrace the instruments had an uplifting effect on Leo. It raised his spirits toward the future. Once he was doing better, my wife, Lucille, and I introduced him to our friend, Phyllis Thomas. Leo liked Phyllis very much. They got along well for many months and decided to marry. On Sept. 20, 1980, they were wed while on board a cruise ship.

Leo and Phyllis Fender sitting on the Great Wall of China.

Leo and Phyllis traveled to many famous historical places of interest to Leo. In particular, he always had a desire to see the Great Wall of China. They made the trip to China, but it was difficult for both of them. There was a lot of walking involved in touring this masterpiece of building technology.

Over the next several years, Leo and Phyllis enjoyed other cruises and G&L operated successfully. The company produced many new electric guitars and bases, and Leo spent a lot of time designing pickups. One regular occurrence was our attendance at the NAMM Show, which was held every year so companies could display their new products. Time passed pretty quickly.

I'll share the highlights of the G&L line here, but for details on each and every instrument, see Part III of this book. In 1982, we built the G-200 guitar, but it was not very long-lived because of its different body style and shorter string length. Also in 1982, we introduced the S-500 guitar, without mini-toggle switches. The S-500 with the mini-toggle switches came much later. That same year the SB-1 and SB-2 basses became a reality.

The El Toro bass, Cavalier guitar, and Nighthawk guitar were finished in 1984. The SC-2 guitar with Strat-style body, as well as the SC-3 with the Strat-style body were also introduced around this time.

Amid this activity, Leo and I encouraged workers to take some R&R. We often had lunch parties so

Richard Smith playing a G&L ASAT guitar at one of the G&L parties.

everyone could become better acquainted. Getting together helped people work more effectively as a team. We also held annual Christmas parties for the employees and their families. Everyone enjoyed these get-togethers. They were an important break in employees' steady workaday lives and they showed the company's appreciation.

In 1985, the great G&L Broadcaster guitar was introduced. It was a popular instrument, but it was only produced for a short period. Retailers were never able to keep up with demand. Even to this day, people still ask where they might get this instrument. The name "Broadcaster" was used on the first Fender guitar, but was dropped when Fender learned that another company was already

Richard Smith and his group playing at one of the G&L Christmas parties.

Buck Owens with the Red, White and Blue G&L guitar that Leo Fender presented to Buck at the Crazy Horse Steak House in Newport Beach, CA, where he was performing (just a short time before Leo passed away).

George and Lucille Fullerton with Buck Owens holding the Red, White and Blue G&L guitar that was given to Buck.

Buck Owens's Crystal Palace in Bakersfield, California.

using that name. Eventually, the name went unused and G&L picked it up again. However, when Fender officials objected to our use of it, we felt obligated to make a change to the name "ASAT" (see origin of name on page 114).

Perhaps the biggest triumph at G&L was the ASAT guitar, created in 1986. It became an instant success. And in 1989, the ASAT bass and the ASAT guitar became a wonderful set of fine musical instruments.

One special memory during my G&L days is of a guitar built for Buck Owens. It was red, white and blue. Leo presented it to Buck during his engagement playing at the Crazy Horse Steakhouse in Newport Beach. After the show was over, we went backstage to see Buck. He was so pleased with the guitar made especially for him that he was overcome emotionally. He sat beside Leo and hugged him. Buck's eyes were full of tears as he told Leo how much he admired him.

In 1990, Leo and I had an idea to create a new instrument that we referred to as a baritone guitar/bass. It was tuned halfway between the guitar and bass. Leo felt this range would help musicians get new and different sounds. He was anxious to complete the prototype instrument and field-test it. That had to be done before we made any tooling to be used in production.

On Tuesday, March 20, 1991, the work was completed on the first unit. That day, it would be polished and completely assembled so that by the next morning Leo could see it when he came in.

Leo never got to see this new instrument. He passed away in the early morning of March 21,

Photo courtesy of Robb Lawrence

This Baratone Bass Guitar is the last instrument that Leo Fender and George Fullerton built before Leo died. It was assembled the day Leo died; he never got to see it. (PG)

1991. That was a sad day for me and music lovers everywhere as news of Leo's death went around the world.

After Leo's death, we designed a special guitar in his memory. It was an ASAT Classic built out of beautifully grained Australian lacewood. The instrument had a gold pickguard and gold hardware. A small gold rose and a copy of Leo's signature were on the upper part of the body. Only seven of these guitars were built. The plan was to build more, but the special wood was not available. Two hundred and fifty commemorative guitars were built using ash bodies. A commemorative ASAT bass was also built.

Chapter 14

BBE Sound Buys G&L

G&L operated until the end of 1991. At that time, the company was sold to settle Leo's estate. BBE Sound Corp., located in Huntington Beach, Calif., bought G&L later that year.

John McLaren, BBE Sound Chief Executive Officer and Chairman of the Board, has vowed to preserve the G&L factory in the same location. John has also retained the original name. "It's G&L Musical Products Inc., just the way Leo Fender established it," John says. (A few articles were written about the name "G&L" being changed to "Guitars by Leo," but this never happened. Someone started this story, and writers who did not check their facts picked it up.)

John McLaren, Jr. is the manager of the factory. His charge is to operate the facility much the same way it ran when Leo was alive. As a testament to BBE's commitment to Leo's legacy, Leo's office and lab are exactly the same as they were his last day. Sometimes they show these rooms to people who tour the facility. They want this part of the memory of Leo to remain unchanged.

Johnny McLaren, Plant Manager, holding a Rampage guitar.

Tony Petrilla, Service Manager.

Doyle Dykes, George Fullerton, and David McLaren.

David McLaren is Executive VP at the company. His plan for G&L is to expand distribution of the products in the United States and foreign countries. This is needed to introduce more prospective customers to the instruments as well as to support the growth of the company.

G&L instruments are gaining acceptance as one of the greater choices for players today. Many players are changing to G&L from other brands of instruments because of the Magnetic Field Design (MFD) pickups Leo designed. The Leo Fender name still has the magic to attract guitar players everywhere.

G&L instruments are also offered in exciting new colors. Since the company began making the instruments in customized colors and trims, the factory has been quite busy. It seems that customers want their instruments to reflect their desire for unique, custom equipment.

Since Leo died, I have not been as active in the guitar business. But BBE Sound has been good to me. As a consultant for G&L, I have the freedom to be out in the field, meeting people in the music business. I appreciate this opportunity to still be a part of the G&L family.

In 1996, G&L designed and produced a George Fullerton signature guitar. They presented the first instrument to me at the 1996 NAMM Show in Anaheim. It had the serial number GF0001.

It is a gorgeous guitar, made in the same style as the original Fender Stratocaster. It has hand-wound pickups and the same wire and wiring dia-

Johnny McLaren, George Fullerton (with original 1985 Broadcaster guitar), John McLaren (with 20th-anniversary ASAT #1), and David McLaren.

gram as the early models. It has been well accepted by customers. Each instrument is shipped with a signed book.

There are many players praising the great sounds they are able to get using G&L instruments. It gives me a good feeling to know that G&L is offering something of great value to the public. Leo would appreciate people enjoying what was his life's work.

George Fullerton and John McLaren.
John is the CEO and Chairman of the Board of BBE, Inc.

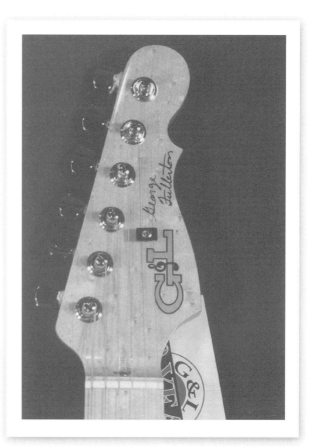

George Fullerton's G&L Signature Guitar, serial #GF0001.

George Fullerton signing 20th-anniversary certificate.

Johnny McLaren signing 20th-anniversary certificate.

Julie at the G&L factory office.

Amanda Ybarra: final assembly of G&L guitars.

Photo courtesy of Dave Kyle

David McLaren and George Fullerton.

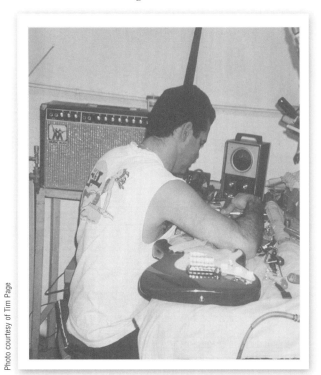

Photo courtesy of Tim Page

Gene Engleheart setting up a new G&L guitar.

Photo courtesy of Tim Page

Ed Sebest, G&L Plant Foreman.

Chapter 15

Building a G&L

The talented people who build G&L instruments today are happy to produce the final product Leo envisioned. Everyone at the factory enjoys being a part of a winning team in the highly competitive instrument-manufacturing business.

The process of creating a G&L guitar is something special. Many of the factory workers are musicians so they bring a special human touch to every instrument. Without their touch and love for great guitars and basses something would be lost.

Many manufacturers are interested in how quickly instruments can be built, without giving much consideration for the quality desired by the players. It seems the main reason for building instruments using fast production methods is to sell more units at a lower price.

This thinking floods the market with second-rate instruments and prevents these instruments from ever being a solid investment for the owner. But the truth of the matter is that more people are interested in the quality of the guitar rather than its price.

That's why many well-known musicians and entertainers recognize the great value that hand-made G&L instruments offer. Buyers are looking for better quality instruments by a reputable manufacturer. And G&L has grown into this position as a highly respected and important part of the electric instrument business.

There is meticulous attention to detail in every phase of building the fabulous G&L instruments. That's why many players praise G&L guitars for their fantastic appearance and superb action and sound. It's like hearing the echo of Leo when he said, "These are the best instruments I've ever built."

Chapter 16
Making Body Blanks

G&L's woodworking shop is quite reminiscent of the early Fender factory. Ed Sebest, who is in charge of G&L production, says several different kinds of wood are used to make guitar bodies, such as lightweight ash, mahogany, alder, and basswood. Flame maple is also used for the tops of special instruments.

All of the wood for making body blanks is brought into the factory in the form of lumber, which has been specially dried and selected for stability. The wood pieces for the body blanks are cut to length and selected for matching wood grain. They are

Photo courtesy of Tim Page

G&L woodshop.

marked to make sure the pieces stay together while they are stored in a drying room until it's time for them to be glued into a block of wood that can be machined into a body blank.

After the machining is done on the blank, the body shape is penciled on the wood, ready for band-sawing the part into shape. After being band-sawed, a routing plate is attached to the

Woodshop

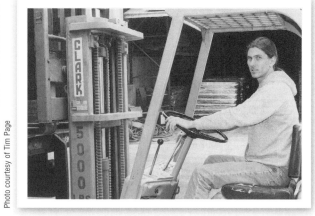

Kenny Amaon

Cutting lumber to make body blanks.

Wood cut and marked for matching (for gluing up body blanks).

Gluing and clamping wood to make body blanks.

blank. A skilled operator does the routing on a high-speed pin router to ensure careful workmanship. After routing, the bodies are passed through a flat belt sander to make sure the proper thickness is maintained.

The bodies are now ready to have all the necessary holes drilled, contours band-sawed, and the edges rounded. After the contours and the rest of the body are sanded on the sanding machines, they are ready to be hand-sanded.

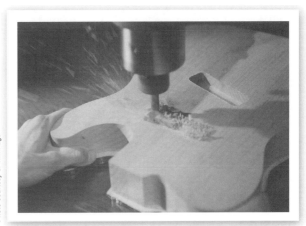

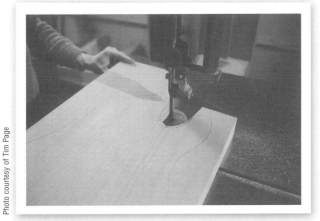

Band-sawing body blanks to shape.

Routing bodies

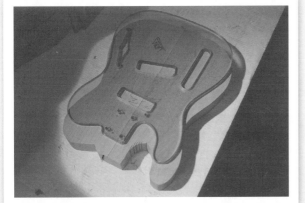

Body and routing plate

Marking the contour shape on the body.

Hand-sanding gives the wood a highly smooth surface. After inspection, they are passed on to the finish department storage area, where they remain for several days in a drying area before the finish is applied.

If the guitar is to have a flame maple top, it goes through a special step after the shaping, contouring and sanding. It is placed into a special gluing machine to fix a piece of contoured flame maple on the top of the body.

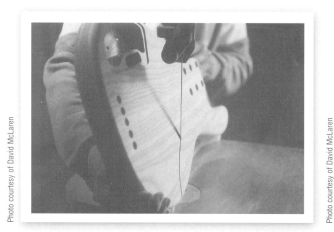

Band-sawing the contour shape of body.

Belt-sanding the contour shape of body.

All of the instrument body blanks are made in the G&L factory. G&L does not use body blanks built by other companies. This gives it better control of instrument quality.

Sanding the contour on a 5-string bass body.

Drum sanding the edge of body.

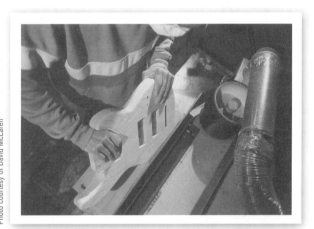

Belt-sanding contour of body.

Drum sanding the body shape.

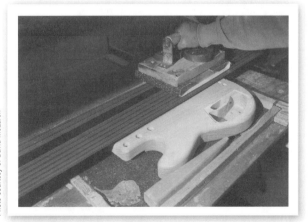

Stroke-sanding the flat surface of body.

Drum sanding the body shape.

Photo courtesy of David McLaren

Fixture for holding a 5-string bass body for stroke sanding.

Photo courtesy of David McLaren

Vacuum tables for gluing wood veneer on bodies.

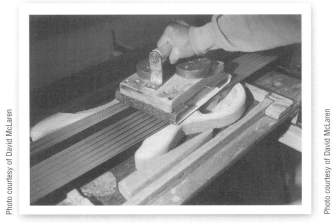

Photo courtesy of David McLaren

Stroke-sanding a 5-string bass body.

Photo courtesy of David McLaren

Vacuum table in operation.

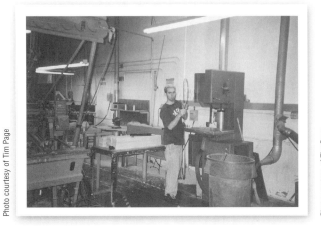

Photo courtesy of Tim Page

G&L woodshop band saw area.

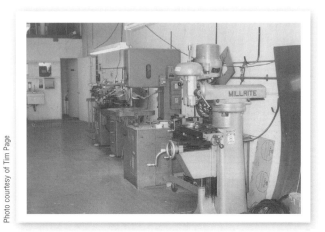

Photo courtesy of Tim Page

Some of the metal-working machines.

Chapter 17
Making Instrument Necks

G&L makes most neck blanks out of hard rock maple and a few out of mahogany. Many necks are all maple, including the fingerboard. Others are made out of maple, but have other kinds of wood for the fingerboard, such as rosewood and ebony. The fingerboard wood on each instrument is determined by the order department.

The hard rock maple lumber is specially dried before it is brought to the factory to be processed. After the wood is cut to length and machined down to a predetermined size, the blank stock is

Photo courtesy of David McLaren

Neck blanks being worked on in the woodshop.

stored in a special room until it is ready to be made into necks.

When the blanks are ready for processing, they are removed from the holding room and inspected to make sure they are straight and in good condition. This is done before machining them to the proper thickness.

Next, the blanks are cut down the center into halves. One of these pieces has a long curving slot routed in the edge to make room for the truss rod. After the truss rod is installed in the slot, the two pieces are carefully glued back together, making sure to keep the glue from getting on the rod.

After the glue is dry, the blank is sanded to make sure the joint is smooth and almost invisible.

I spent a lot of time trying to determine the best method of installing truss rods. Leo and I finally settled on this approach after getting this design tested, approved and patented. G&L is the only company that uses this superior way of installing truss rods.

Next, the neck shape is penciled on the sanded blank. After the neck is sawed by hand into shape, a routing plate is attached to blank and it is routed all around the outside shape on a high-speed pin router.

After the outside of the neck is routed, the back of the neck is run on a shaper to rough out the shape while leaving enough material for the final shaping and sanding, which will be done later.

The headstock is machined to proper thickness and all of the holes are drilled for the installation of tuners. The fingerboard has all of the holes drilled for the upper position markers. The position markers are then inlaid.

Making necks in the woodshop.

Photo courtesy of David McLaren

Bi-cut necks being assembled in the woodshop.

G&L woodshop: large belt sander and large planer.

The binding on the edge of the fingerboard on some necks has to be applied before the oval radius is cut and sanded on the fingerboard. While the neck is still on the same fixture, saw slots will be cut for inserting the metal frets.

After the frets are installed, the fret wire ends will be cut off on each side of the fingerboard. This procedure is the same on all fingerboards whether

Rows of necks with and without fingerboards.

Installing truss rods in neck blanks.

Eddie Gomez shaping guitar neck headstock.

Gluing neck blanks together after truss rod has been installed.

Manny Beorin sanding guitar neck headstock.

81

they are on an all-maple neck or made out of a special wood. After the fretting is completed, the bone nut is installed.

The neck is now ready to go through all of the careful sanding stages to get the proper shape and feel before it is inspected and accepted in the holding room for the finish department. This final step in making a guitar neck requires highly

Installing side-position markers on fingerboard.

Attaching fixture to a 5-string bass neck to prepare it for cutting of the fret slots.

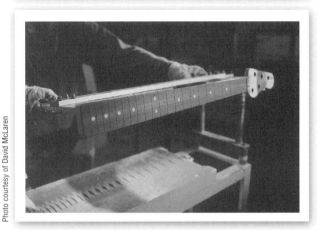

Sawing slots in fingerboard for installing frets.

Cutting fret slots on a 5-string bass neck.

Installing frets on a neck.

trained people. Most of the people who do the final sanding on the necks are guitar players themselves, so they already know how a professional guitar neck should feel.

G&L uses the tried and proven method of having people—not machines—do all of the intricate and important stages of shaping and completing instruments. People provide a touch of love and the fine workmanship that is apparent in every G&L instrument.

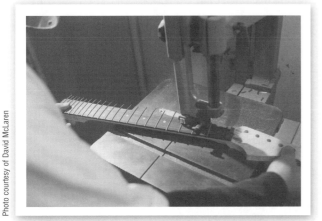

Sanding the oval on top of fingerboard.

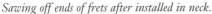

Sawing off ends of frets after installed in neck.

Sanding the oval sape of the fingerboard of a 5-string-bass neck.

Photo courtesy of Tim Page

Mike D'Angelo shaping the radius of the guitar neck.

Photo courtesy of Tim Page

Nathan Conrad drilling holes for controls.

Photo courtesy of Tim Page

Reno gluing fingerboards on neck blanks.

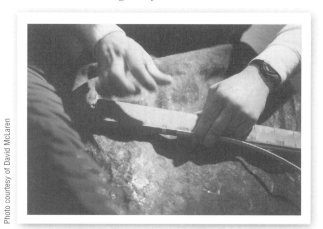

Photo courtesy of David McLaren

Photo courtesy of Tim Page

Neck blanks with fingerboards glued on.

Photo courtesy of David McLaren

Gluing binding on necks.

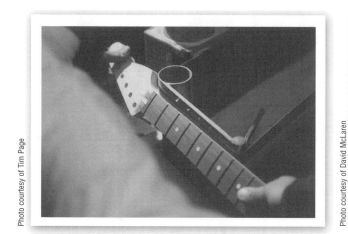

Photo courtesy of Tim Page

Sanding the backside of the neck.

Photo courtesy of David McLaren

Photo courtesy of David McLaren

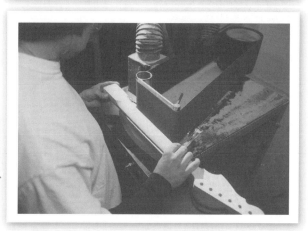

Photo courtesy of David McLaren

Sanding the back of the neck.

Photo courtesy of David McLaren

Drum sanding the headstock.

Chapter 18

Putting the Finish On

The bodies from the woodshop are placed in a warm room where the environment is carefully controlled to allow the wood to stabilize. After several days, each body is removed and carefully inspected for cracks in the glue joints or any other changes in the wood. This makes certain the body is in perfect condition before the finish is applied.

G&L instruments have a special appearance and luster that comes from the way the colors are blended with clear polyester. The many colors available are the product of well-trained and talented people who create these masterpieces. The most popular finishes are G&L's premier see-through finishes, which includes the sunburst style. They highlight the beautiful woods used as well as add color.

The polyester finishes are carefully applied in a dust-free, controlled atmosphere, to ensure the best possible results. After they receive several coats of finish and water sanding with fine grit sandpaper between coats, the bodies are placed in

G&L instrument color chart. (PG)

Finishing department

a drying and holding room for several days before they are ready to be polished. When they are ready for polishing, they are removed and inspected to be sure they are still in good condition. They are sanded lightly and receive the final special hand-polishing that gives them a fantastic luster. After the polishing process is complete, the bodies are placed in a protective container until they are ready for final assembly. The special attention given to the finishing process on all instruments has earned G&L acclaim for having the most beautiful colors and finishes in the music industry.

Putting gun-oil tint finish on neck.

Necks with gun-oil tint finish.

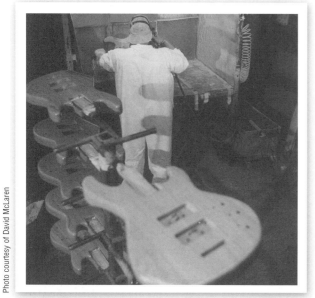

Spraying finish on an L-2000 bass body.

Spraying finish on an L-2000 bass body.

The finishing process for the necks is similar to the process used on the bodies. First, the necks are placed in a warm holding room for several days. The environment is controlled to allow the wood to stabilize. Storing the necks in this special holding room is essential to be sure they do not change in any way that would cause them to be faulty.

After the necks are removed from this room, they are carefully inspected to be certain they are in good condition. Then they are moved to the finishing department, where a coat of polyurethane is applied to each neck.

The polyurethane completely covers the all-maple neck and fingerboard, including the frets.

The frets are sanded later to remove the coating, so the strings will come in contact with the metal frets directly. The necks with rosewood or ebony

Painter Hector Melgoza painting a black Comanche.

Spraying finish on the body.

Painter Malcolm McLarmore doing another famous G&L burst finish.

Spray booths

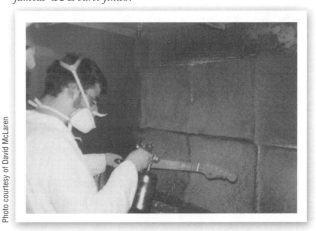

Spencer Brown spraying final clear coat on neck.

fingerboards do not have the finish sprayed on top of the fingerboard and frets.

It takes a lot of careful light sanding and hand-buffing to get the high-gloss luster that is required on all necks with polyurethane finish. Before necks are accepted in the assembly department, it is essential that the necks are smooth and have just the right feel for the player's hand. After the necks are polished, they are placed in a protective container and moved into the final assembly area.

Efrain Meraz is a supervisor in finish-polishing, which is all done by hand.

Polishing the finish on a 5-string bass body.

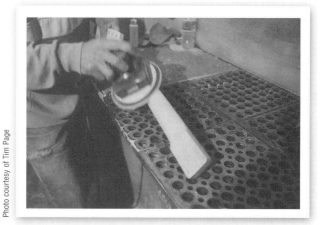

Hand-sanding the necks.

Chapter 19
Building Great Pickups

Pickups are the heart of every guitar, so they must be built to the highest standard of excellence. G&L achieves excellence in its MFD pickups using hand-winding coil machines, which create better-sounding pickups than those made with machine-wound coils. The machines were designed and built by Leo in the company machine shop.

The winders are made using a sewing machine motor and foot control. They are driven by rubber band belts to turn the pulleys. A rubber band is also used to operate the turn counter.

The secret for superior coil winding on long and narrow coil forms is to keep the coil wire tight all the way around the form as it is turned. This tension is accomplished by the stretching and the reciprocating action of the rubber band belts. Without this action, the coil wire would be loose on the sides and tight over the ends.

One of the most intricate operations is building the pickup coil form and preparing it for the hand-winding of the enamel-coated coil wire. The people who do the hand-winding are highly trained for this work. They hold the small diameter coil wire carefully between the thumb and index finger. As the form rotates on the machine, they guide the wire into the channel of the coil form. This

requires steady nerves and a tremendous amount of tenacity. Hand-winding creates crisscrossing of the coil wire as it is wound on the form. The small openings between the crisscrossing of the coil wire allow the magnetic field to more completely saturate the coil, therefore changing the capacitance of the coil, which gives the pickup more power and a cleaner, stronger signal from the strings.

After the pickup coils are wound and inspected, the lead wires are soldered onto the coils. The coils are checked for proper function again. Some of the pickups are wrapped with cotton string and

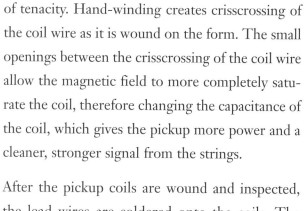

Making pickup coil forms

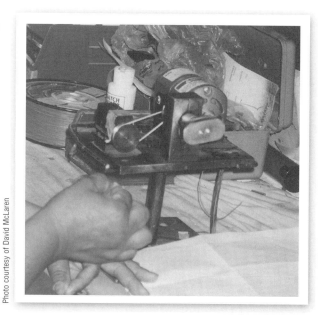

Shug Atkinson, my sister, winding coils for G&L pickups.

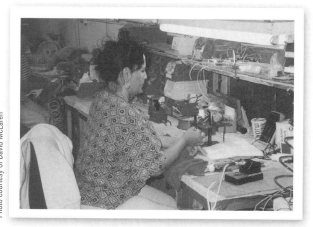

Isela Ramos hand-winding coils for G&L guitar pickups.

all pickups are dipped into wax to eliminate microphonic noise.

The MFD magnets are charged before attachment to the coils. Now they are ready to be installed in a guitar. The MFD pickups with adjustable pole pieces used on G&L guitars are the finest pickups available on instruments today.

Hand-winding coils for G&L pickups. Note the careful and accurate handling of the very fine copper wire.

Hand-winding coils for G&L pickups. Note the shiny fine copper wire being wound on the pickup form.

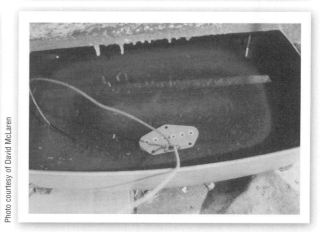

Dipping the pickup in hot wax.

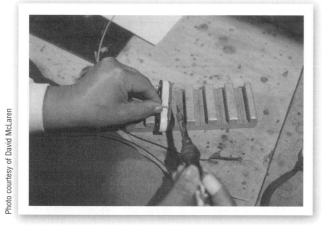

Soldering leads on pickup.

Completed pickup

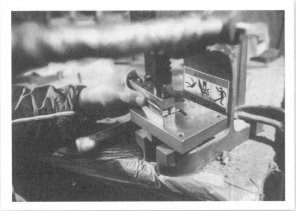

Photo courtesy of David McLaren

Making pickup coil forms.

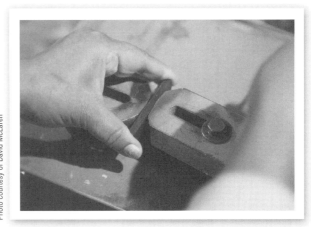

Photo courtesy of David McLaren

Charging magnets.

Photo courtesy of David McLaren

Carmen Guiterez working with guitar pickups and pickguards.

Photo courtesy of Tim Page

Virginia Dias putting pickups into covers.

Chapter 20

Gathering Other Parts, Entering Final Assembly

There are lots of other parts needed to complete an instrument, and these must be made ahead of the time so they will be ready when the instrument reaches final assembly. The bridge alone has many parts to enable the tuning of each string to the proper height and length for the best intonation. And depending on the model of the guitar, some bridges have a vibrato unit as part of the assembly and others do not.

The control plate is assembled with the proper controls, knobs, and switches. The wiring is done on a workbench, soldering the components together. The hookup wire is cotton pushback insulation, just like the kind used in the early Fender guitars.

When all the parts are available to assemble a new instrument, several people help in the building process. Some workers install the parts on the body and others install the neck and strings. When the assembly is complete, the instrument is placed on a special rack for final testing.

The final testing is a specialized process. The strings are tuned and every other part of the instrument is adjusted to a specific set of rules. The string height at the nut must be set to the designated depth, and the string length adjusted for perfect sound intonation. The height of the bridge saddles is also adjusted to have the exact string clearance when the string is held down against the first and last fret on the fingerboard. This clearance space is critical in having the right action.

G&L final assembly

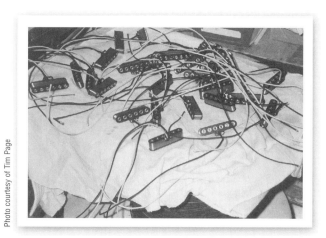

Waxed pickups for magnet installation.

Amanda Ybarra, final assembly.

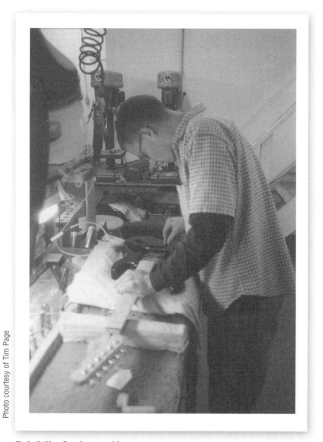

Rob Sills, final assembly.

The people who do the final testing are all professional guitar players so they understand how the neck and action must feel to be accepted by other players. When all the adjustments are made and the instrument is in tune, the instrument must be played to make sure the action is smooth on the strings and all parts are working well. The tester must be sure the controls and switches are work-

Final assembly department

Rack of strings ready to be used on new instruments.

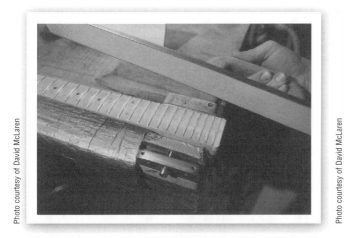

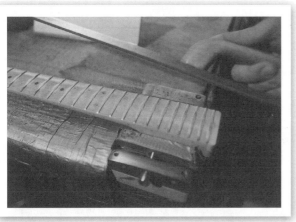

Preparing frets on necks to be ready for final assembly.

Filing and sanding frets on neck to be ready for final assembly.

Joe Giurbino polishing one of the hand-rubbed oil tint necks.

Preparing necks for final assembly.

ing the way they are supposed to, and the tone and volume of the sound is acceptable. The true test is asking himself if he would be satisfied with the results if he were buying this instrument.

If he is pleased with the results after this rigorous testing procedure, he passes it along to be inspected and placed into a container to be cleaned and packaged. G&L packs its guitars in special cartons designed to protect the instrument during shipping. Everyone takes care in handling these great instruments to insure they will be in the best possible condition when received by

Ken is inspecting before shipment of instrument.

music retailers. The retailers often say that G&L guitars are still in tune and ready to be played when they reach the store.

I take great pleasure in knowing retailers around the world are getting the best handmade instruments possible. Everyone at G&L feels privileged to work

at one of the few companies that still produces an American-made product. Comparatively speaking, there are very few companies that have not taken their products overseas to be built at a lower price.

G&L strives to maintain the pride in manufacturing established many years ago, when Leo

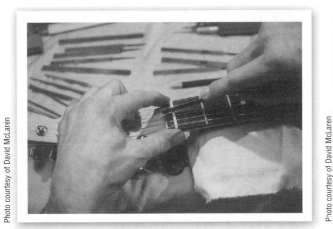
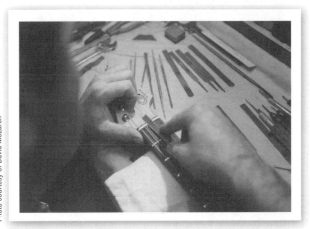

Filing slots on bone nut for string height.

Completed instruments

Final assembly department

99

insisted on building instruments to the highest possible level of quality. Leo's spirit of achievement still exists and remains a guiding force in everyone who is involved with G&L and its mission to build the best guitars in the world.

Final inspection of an ASAT Deluxe.

Setup of an S-500.

Kenny Amaon making final check before packing a new G&L guitar.

Gene Engleheart setting up a new G&L guitar.

Photo courtesy of David McLaren

Final testing an S-500.

Photo courtesy of David McLaren

Final inspection of an ASAT Deluxe.

Photo courtesy of David McLaren

Bridge height adjustment on an S-500.

Shipping area for instruments.

PART III

A Detailed History
of G&L Instruments

Lots of guitar and bass enthusiasts want to understand the evolution of

G&L instruments from their beginning to today. Here's a chronological review

of when certain instruments where made and what went into them.

Chapter 21
The First G&L Guitars and Basses

When MusicMan started cutting its orders, the writing was on the wall. We knew we would have to build our own instruments to keep operating our factory efficiently. By the late '70s, we were developing new designs for our own line. By 1979, we had almost completed work on the MFD pickup, the Saddle-Lock bridge and Dual-Fulcrum vibrato. By early 1980, the designs were complete.

We turned our attention to integrating these features into a line of instruments. Once again, Leo and I had designed Fender guitars, then evolved those into the MusicMan designs. With G&L, we took another step forward in guitar and bass design to suit how music was evolving and expanding. Musical styles were blending—with country music mixing with rock, mixing with blues, mixing with funk, and so on.

Leo and I spent a lot of time talking to musicians about what they wanted in their instruments. They wanted more versatility. A lot of guitarists, for example, needed to get a variety of tones, but

Photo courtesy of David McLaren

L-2000 bass

Photo courtesy of Tim Page

1981 fretless L-2000 bass (PG)

the only way to do this was by using several guitars at every gig. We set out to make a guitar with lots of good, usable tones.

In some ways, we had accomplished this with the MusicMan Stingray guitar. However, with the new MFD humbucker and electronics, the first G&L guitar, the F-100, could really deliver a lot of versatility. It could cover almost any situation, from hard rock to blues to country. But to get the most out of this design, we built a preamp system for the F-100.

The first G&L bass, the L-1000, had a single MFD humbucking pickup and passive electronics. The design goal of the L-1000 was to fill a gap between the old Precision bass design, the Stingray, and the Sabre bass. The Stingray and the Sabre both had modern sounds, but there was still high demand for

the Precision bass. Musicians told us they really liked the Precision but wanted a more powerful tone. The L-1000 fit in quite well with Precision players, plus the Saddle-Lock bridge helped give better sustain and improve the definition of notes. Within a few months of the L-1000, we completed the L-2000 and L-2000E, which had two MFD humbucking pickups. The L-2000E had active electronics, not to add power to the already hot pickups, but to get more tones. Compared with the Sabre bass, the MFD pickups had a better sound, plus the preamp design in the L-2000 enhanced versatility. These electronic improvements plus the new Saddle-Lock bridge took our two-humbucking-pickup concept of the Sabre bass to a whole new level in the L-2000E. In 1989, G&L introduced a Leo Fender signature model of the L-2000.

Chapter 22
The Innovative G-200

In the early '80s, the Gibson Les Paul was popular. But players complained about the instrument's weight. One guy said, "It is like carrying an anvil around your neck." So I thought we should build a better Les Paul. The design goal was to make a G&L that sounded better and was more comfortable than a Les Paul. Thus, the G-200 was born. We already had a versatile two-humbucking guitar in the F-100, so I designed the G-200 around the pickups in the F-100 and used the 24¾-inch scale length of the Les Paul.

Instead of using the preamp and control circuit of the F-100 II, the control layout of the G-200 was close to that of a Les Paul. The G-200 also had the benefit of the Saddle-Lock bridge, which gave better sustain and tone compared with a Les Paul bridge.

Leo wasn't pleased with the instrument or its short scale. He liked the 25½-inch scale much better. Though he went along with it, he insisted on the instrument having a control plate. I drew up some control plates with coaching from Leo, and the end result was the "cloud shape."

I really didn't want to have a control plate on the G-200, and after the dealers told us players didn't want it either, Leo gave in and allowed the G-200 to have controls mounted through the rear. In fact, a lot of dealers complained about G&Ls having controls plates, asking us to mount the controls from the rear.

Leo didn't like the G-200 from the beginning, and after we changed to rear-mounted controls, he disliked it even more. Every time we got orders for G-200s, Leo would talk about the design and why he didn't like it. Though I liked the guitar, it wasn't worth upsetting Leo. The G-200 was the only G&L guitar to have a 24¾-inch scale length. We made the G-200 for less than two years before it was discontinued.

Chapter 23

The Evolution of the S-500

The S-500 was G&L's first attempt to evolve the Stratocaster. It was natural that dealers and musicians would ask us to design a better Stratocaster. The Strat was our most famous design, so people expected we would pick up where we left off.

When we started G&L, we wanted to see how far we could push the envelope in design and versatility, but we also saw an opportunity to improve the basic Fender designs we'd done nearly 30 years before. Up to this point, we only made guitars and basses with humbucking MFD pickups. The MFD design, however, worked equally well in a single-coil pickup. We designed a single-coil MFD pickup to appeal to Strat players. This new MFD single-coil pickup, coupled with the benefits of the Dual-Fulcrum vibrato, made the S-500 sound stronger and more melodic. It had more midrange and warmth, and less harshness compared with a Strat pickup. By this time we also had a new, patented truss rod design in the Bi-Cut neck, which I have discussed elsewhere in this book.

Nighthawk/Skyhawk

By the following year, we decided to change the pickup from the rectangular shape of the early S-500 to a traditional Strat shape and size. This allowed us to begin selling MFD single-coil pickups in the aftermarket, so Strat players could upgrade their guitars to come close to the sound of a G&L. We introduced these pickups in a new model called the Nighthawk, which was very much like S-500. However, we changed from a metal pickguard to a plastic one. We were trying to make it play, feel, and look more like a Stratocaster than the early S-500 did.

1985 blonde Skyhawk—personal guitar of Tim Page (PG)

Shortly after we introduced the Nighthawk, we found out there was a band named Nighthawk. We made contact with them to see if there we could use the name, and they said we couldn't. So we renamed the instrument Skyhawk. In 1987, we changed the Skyhawk, making the body a little more contemporary as well as mounting the controls in the pickguard instead of a separate metal control plate. We relocated the input jack from the control plate mount to a separate angled input jack like on a Strat. We also changed the headstock design from the typical G&L design to what people call the "sickle" shape. This late version of the Skyhawk didn't have the trademark G&L "hook" in it. In our opinion, this made the guitar look like a more modern Stratocaster.

In 1989, we introduced a Leo Fender signature version of the Skyhawk, which was the same as the standard Skyhawk except for the Leo Fender decal on the body.

Modern S-500/S-500 Signature

When we started G&L, we tried very hard to keep the instruments from looking like Fenders. If they looked similar, we thought people would say we copied Fender and not realize the many engineering improvements we made. We felt they had to look different so people would see that these guitars were different. However, over the years, G&L gained recognition and a reputation, so we began to feel more comfortable adding Fender design elements. Once we came out with the ASAT Classic in 1987, people immediately started pressuring us to make a guitar that looked almost the same as a Stratocaster. The Nighthawk had evolved to look more like a Strat, but they wanted a G&L Stratocaster.

Dale and I got a lot of feedback from people asking for such a guitar. While we had in mind to keep G&Ls looking different from Fenders, it seems people didn't want that. Since it was our goal to make instruments people wanted, we decided not to let our concern get in the way. The important thing was that the engineering improvements we developed at G&L be appreciated and enjoyed by as many musicians as possible. In 1989, we introduced the modern S-500. It had the body shape, pickguard shape and overall styling of a Strat, but was still a G&L in every sense. It had the MFD single-coil pickups, Dual-Fulcrum vibrato, Bi-Cut neck, our treble and bass controls, and even a mini-toggle to allow combinations of neck and bridge pickups or all three pickups together. That same year we introduced a Leo Fender signature version of the S-500, which was the same as the standard S-500 except for the Leo Fender decal on the body.

Cavalier

The Cavalier was introduced in 1983 using the same body as the Nighthawk and early Skyhawk. It had a similar three-ply black pickguard, black metal control plate, a three-position pickup selector, standard Dual-Fulcrum vibrato, single volume, and two tone controls. The Cavalier was different in that it had two offset MFD humbuckers, the same as those offered in the original X-body Interceptor. The Cavalier wasn't accepted well, and I'm not sure if people didn't like the look of those pickups or if they didn't like the sound.

Photo courtesy of Mark Burroughs and Tim Page

Black Comanche guitar

Comanche

In 1987, we introduced the Comanche, which was the most radical evolution of the Stratocaster concept. It had three Z-coil pickups, which were marketed as "single-coil humbuckers." They were essentially split-coil pickups with one coil for the upper three strings and another for the lower three strings. Each coil was wound in opposite directions, and each pickup had four wire leads so that each coil could be turned on or off independently. The Comanche had a total of six mini-toggle switches: three of them were two-position switches to turn each pickup on or off, and the other three were three-position switches to control the coils of each pickup. A three-position mini-toggle could switch on one coil, the other coil or both coils. With the ability to turn on or off each pickup, as well as turn on or off each coil of each pickup, the range of tones in the Comanche was amazing. The pickups themselves sounded beautiful, with clear highs, warm lows, high output, and no noise. The only problem was that this original Comanche model, known as the Comanche VI among collectors, was challenging to use. It was difficult enough to use in a live situation, but even more difficult for dealers to explain to customers.

The solution came in the Comanche V, which eliminated the six mini-toggles in favor of a traditional five-position pickup selector and a single mini-toggle. The single mini-toggle could be used to get a neck and bridge combination, or all three pickups on. Though there was no longer the ability to control each coil of each pickup, the Comanche V was easy to use and sold much better. The Comanche V had a volume control, a treble control, and a bass control, while the Comanche VI had a volume control, and a treble control. The Comanche of today has the same control arrangement of the Comanche V.

In 1989, Leo Fender signature versions of both Comanche V and Comanche VI were introduced. They were the same as the non-signature models, except for the signature decals on the bodies.

Chapter 24

The ASAT

Our first Telecaster-style instrument shared only the Telecaster body style and control plate style. The Broadcaster, introduced in 1985, was clearly targeted at Tele players, but was unlike anything they'd seen before. It used our 22 fret Bi-Cut neck, but other differences were more obvious, including our Saddle-Lock bridge and pickguard. But the pickups were probably the most distinctive difference. They had very shallow, wide bobbins, so the windings stacked up such that they fanned out from the pole pieces. The Broadcaster pickups were entirely different from Telecaster pickups.

We had used these pickups in the SC-2 student model guitar since 1982. In the meantime, we found that Tele players had bought SC-2 guitars because the SC-2s had similar tonal qualities to Telecasters, but sounded bigger and fatter. Therefore, we thought it would be interesting to

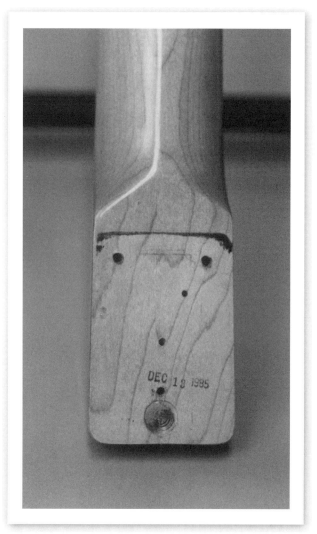

Broadcaster guitar (PG)

Broadcaster neck, dated 12-13-85. (PG)

build a Telecaster-shape guitar using the distinctive G&L features from the SC-2. The Broadcaster was a repackaged SC-2, with a professional appearance to appeal directly to Telecaster players because of the familiar shape and control layout.

We picked the Broadcaster name since it was already famous but seemed out of use for a long time. Our lawyer checked on the name and thought it was clear to use. We filed for a trademark on the Broadcaster name in April 1985. Later in the year, we met opposition to our use of the name. Leo told me that

Fender officials said they thought it was unfair that we should use the name when they had to drop it more than 30 years before. It turned out that Gretsch still had a trademark on Broadcaster for drum kits, but I don't know if Gretsch lawyers filed opposition to our application for the Broadcaster trademark. Even if Fender had not complained to us about the name, Gretsch could have stopped it—just like they did with Fender around 1951.

The Broadcaster name was changed to ASAT in 1986. We had named several models after military artillery, and "A-SAT" is military shorthand for

Neck socket of Broadcaster guitar, inspected and signed by Leo Fender, 1-2-86. (PG)

Photo courtesy of Jeff Byrd and Tim Page

Blonde 1986 ASAT guitar with two single-coil pickups. (PG)

an "anti-satellite" missile. Richard Smith suggested the name ASAT. It seemed good at the time, but many people don't have any idea what it means. I've heard a lot folklore about our choice of ASAT. The most common story is that it stands for "After Strat After Tele." The truth is that ASAT just fit into our use of military names. We thought military names conveyed the best of American strength, precision, and technology.

In 1988, we added a Leo Fender signature model ASAT, which had chrome hardware, white pickup covers, and a white powder-coated metal pickguard.

ASAT Classic/ASAT Classic Signature

In 1987, we were getting so many requests for a "traditional" Telecaster-style instrument that we decided it was time to bring one to market. The ASAT Classic was a traditional Telecaster-style guitar, but also different in many ways. The

ASAT Classic, like all G&Ls, had 22 frets as opposed to Fender's 21 frets, the Bi-Cut neck, and a pickguard shape reminiscent of the ASAT to distinguish it from a Telecaster.

When we were making the ASAT Classic, I took my 1953 Telecaster engineering drawings to our tool-and-die maker and asked for a bridge plate of the same specifications. One change was that we wanted six saddles instead of three (two strings per saddle) as on the old Telecaster. Our saddles were the same shape and style as the early ones, just shorter in width since we were using six. This

115

ASAT Classic in bluburst color finish.

G&L ASAT classic guitar with gold hardware, vibrato, and Leo Fender signature on body.

allowed better intonation of the strings, but still offered the same tone that a traditional Telecaster bridge offered.

The most important element that made the ASAT Classic a G&L instead of a Fender copy was our MFD versions of the Telecaster pickups. In fact, the ASAT Classic pickups could be retro-fitted into a Telecaster. For a few years, G&L sold the ASAT Classic pickups as "Telecaster replace-ments." The MFD pickups gave ASAT Classics a fatter, warmer sound, yet still retained the punchy, twangy sound that Teles were known for.

The neck pickup had quite a bit more output than a Tele neck pickup, too.

Cosmetically, the ASAT Classic bridge pickup looked just like a vintage Telecaster pickup except for the adjustable pole pieces. The ASAT Classic neck pickup did away with the chrome-plated brass cover in favor of a plastic cover exposing the adjustable pole pieces. We used different wire for the ASAT Classic pickups, as well as a different number of winds.

Photo courtesy of Tim Page

Black ASAT III guitar with two MFD single-coil and one MFD humbucker pickups. (PG)

Photo courtesy of Tim Page

Jazz player Peter Padua with his G&L ASAT III guitar.

ASAT III/ASAT III Signature

Introduced in 1987, the ASAT III was basically an ASAT outfitted with Skyhawk pickups (same as used in the modern S-500) and a five-way pickup selector. In all other respects, the ASAT III was the same as the ASAT, including the black powder-coated hardware and pickguard.

It was designed to satisfy a demand among certain players. At the time, more country players were switching to Stratocasters, but were interested in a Telecaster-style guitar with Strat pickups. These players were used to the feel of a Tele body and neck, but wanted to get a Strat sound.

In 1989, we added a Leo Fender signature version of the ASAT III, which, like other signature models, had chrome hardware, white pickup covers, and a white powder-coated metal pickguard.

Our fears that people would think we copied the Telecaster were unfounded. The ASAT Classic was very appealing to Telecaster players, as we had hoped. A number of Tele players told me that after they bought an ASAT Classic, they almost never played their old Teles anymore.

In 1990, we added a Leo Fender signature model ASAT Classic, which shared the same chrome hardware, white pickup covers, and white powder-coated metal pickguard as the standard ASAT Classic.

1987 ASAT III in natural ash body.

Chapter 25
G&L Rock Guitars

In the early '80s, G&L was focused on designing guitars that suited the music of the day, with many models being "rock" guitars. The Stratocaster had been very popular for decades, and many guitars at the time were souped up versions of Strats. I suppose that's where the term "Super Strat" came from. The market wanted humbuckers, locking vibratos, and slick body shapes. Even country music players were switching to Strats.

When Leo and I talked to musicians about what they wanted, we realized that we needed to address what was happening at the time, instead of just applying our engineering improvements to the traditional Fender models.

Interceptor

We introduced the Interceptor in 1983. It was a truly wild-looking guitar, from its body and head-stock shape to its two-tone color scheme. At the time, a lot of cutting-edge guitars were selling because of rock music and the influence of rock bands' wild appearances. Gibson's Flying V and Explorer were all the rage in the early '80s. Other manufacturers, such as BC Rich, made even wilder guitars.

We needed to address this market with a flamboyant guitar that would really stand out. Leo and I had differences of opinion on how far to take the styling. Leo was opposed to anything that didn't seem "normal" to him. So I drew up some concepts including the X-body design. I wasn't sure I even liked it, but I was trying to find something attractive to the market and good for sales.

We offered the Interceptor X-body with either three MFD single-coil pickups or two offset MFD humbuckers and our Dual-Fulcrum vibrato. The single coils were the same as in the SC-3 and Skyhawk, and the offset humbuckers were the same in the Cavalier. Basically, the X-body was functionally the same as an SC-3 or Cavalier, but in a wild-looking package. However, the rock guitar market was becoming dominated with full-size humbucker guitars and Kahler vibratos.

The Interceptor body shape was revised shortly thereafter. The new shape had more curves, with slimmer and rounder horns to allow easier access to the upper frets. This version of the Interceptor was available with either two MFD single-coil pickups and one full-size Schaller humbucker or two Schaller humbuckers as well as a Kahler vibrato. The SSH version had a volume and single tone control, and each pickup had its own on/off mini-toggle switch. The two-humbucker version had a single pickup selector, volume, and two tone controls (one for each pickup).

The offset humbuckers on the original Interceptor didn't have enough output for the hard rock market, and though we could have used the larger MDF humbuckers from the F-100, the musicians wanted a standard-size humbucker so they could install the one they wanted, for example, from DiMarzio or Seymour Duncan. At this time, we decided all of our rock guitars should use standard full-size humbuckers, as in the two-humbucker version of the revised Interceptor, since that's what the rock guitar market demanded.

In 1988, the Interceptor was revised again, to a more traditional body shape with a rounded lower bout replacing the X-shape. This was the final version of the Interceptor. It features two MFD single-coil pickups and a Schaller humbucker in the bridge position. It has a volume and single tone control, and each pickup had its own on/off mini-toggle switch. The available bridges were the Dual-Fulcrum vibrato with fine tuners, standard Dual-Fulcrum vibrato or Kahler vibrato. Throughout each generation of the Interceptor, the flamboyant two-tone paint scheme remained.

Rampage

Even while we were producing wild-looking Interceptors, we saw that some rockers wanted clean and contemporary guitars. Eddie Van Halen made many players want a stripped-down guitar with one humbucker, a volume control, and a hot-rod vibrato. Kahler vibratos were popular, so they were often used on the "Super Strat" guitars of the time. Our dedicated rock guitar, the Rampage, was introduced in 1984 and came only with a single Schaller humbucker, a volume control, and a Kahler vibrato. It was stripped down to do noth-

1985 black Superhawk with ebony fingerboard and Kahler vibrato. (PG)

1986 red Invader with Kahler vibrato. (PG)

ing but what the hard rocker wanted, and it did it very well. Some years later, I heard that Jerry Cantrell made the Rampage his guitar of choice.

Superhawk

A few months later, we introduced the Superhawk, which was similar to the Rampage, but had two Schaller humbuckers, a pickup selector, and two tone controls (one for each pickup). The Superhawk was for the rocker who needed more versatility. It fit in well with the growing market for two-humbucker rock guitars with bolt-on necks and 25½-inch scale.

Invader

The Invader was introduced at about the same time as the Rampage and Superhawk. It shared the body and neck design with these models. The Invader had two MFD single coils in the neck and middle positions, the same pickups used in the Skyhawk and SC-3, and a Schaller humbucker bridge pickup. It had a volume and single tone control, and each pickup had its own on/off mini-toggle switch. The bridge was usually a Kahler vibrato, but some were made with the Dual-Fulcrum vibrato with fine tuners and G&L locking nut.

Chapter 26

SC and HG Models: The Student Range

In 1982, G&L introduced a range of lower-priced student guitars that still featured the advanced engineering of the higher-priced models. The initial bodies had simple shapes without arm or rear contours, and the upper horns were shaped halfway between a Stratocaster and a Telecaster. The upper horn, particularly, was more Tele-like, but slightly deeper cut. The guitars were later updated with upper horn sculpting more like Strats, in that they were cut more deeply than before.

The SC range originally consisted of three models, SC-1, SC-2 and SC-3, and all came with standard saddle-lock bridges or a Dual-Fulcrum vibrato, as well as simple controls with plastic knobs mounted on a control plate. The SC-1 had only one pickup, an MFD single-coil in the bridge position, and a volume and tone control. The SC-2 had the same bridge pickup, but added a single-coil MFD pickup in the neck position for

1986 rare maroon SC-3 guitar with gold hardware and without pickguard. (PG)

1989 black SC-3 guitar with pickguard signed by George Fullerton. (PG)

a wider range of tones. The SC-2 had a three-position pickup selector, and a volume and tone control. The SC-2 pickup in the neck position became the inspiration for the Broadcaster/ASAT once we discovered how much Telecaster players like the SC-2's tone. Finally, the SC-3 had three MFD single-coil pickups as used in the Skyhawk, with a five-position pickup selector, volume control, and tone control.

When the bodies of the SC range were revised, the SC-1 was dropped and the HG-2 took its place. The HG-2 was the same as an SC-2, except the pickups were MFD humbucking units. These particular MFD humbuckers were not offset, as in the Interceptor and Cavalier, and were used as standard in the HG-2. There were, however, a few ASATs made with this humbucker in the bridge position, though we didn't officially offer ASATs with this pickup.

Chapter 27

G&L Basses in the '80s

SB-1 and SB-2:
The "Standard Bass" Range

In 1982, we wanted to make affordably priced basses comparable to the Precision bass and Jazz bass. The original SB-1 and SB-2 were conceptually similar to the SC range of guitars, in that the bodies had no arm contour or rear contour, passive electronics, simple controls, and plastic knobs.

The original SB-1 had one bi-pole single-coil pickup and single volume and tone controls mounted in a black powder-coated metal control plate. Shortly thereafter, the SB-1 was revised to use a single split-coil bi-pole MFD humbucker, which was basically an MFD version of a split-coil Precision bass pickup. Unlike the SC guitars, the later SB-1 had a black powder-coated metal pickguard, which housed the pickup and controls. Later on, the SB-1 gained body contours, metal knobs, a three-ply plastic pickguard, and the contemporary G&L headstock.

1984 SB-2 bass (PG)

Later SB-2 bass

The original SB-2 had two single-coil bi-pole single-coil pickups, single volume and tone controls, as well as a three-position pickup selector, all with plastic knobs, mounted in a black powder-coated metal control plate. The original SB-2 evolved into a P/J pickup combination, with the SB-1's MFD split coil in the neck position and an MFD single-coil in the bridge position. Basically, the neck pickup was swapped for the SB-1 unit. The revised SB-2 gained body contours, metal knobs, a three-ply plastic pickguard, and the contemporary G&L headstock, just as the SB-1 did.

Lynx

The original SB-2 lived on in the Lynx, introduced in 1984. The Lynx was the same, except for body contours and the contemporary G&L headstock.

El Toro

The El Toro was introduced in 1982, and appeared like an L-2000, but with two bi-pole humbucking pickups in place of the two large single-pole MFD humbuckers used in the L-2000. The El Toro's switching and active circuitry were also different.

Cosmetically, the El Toro and L-2000 shared a body shape. But when the L-2000's controls were rear-mounted in the late '80s, the El Toro continued with front-loaded controls mounted to a black powder-coated metal plate.

Interceptor

In 1983, the El Toro's electronics were packaged in a wild-looking, two-tone body, which mirrored the revised Interceptor guitar. The Interceptor bass also used the sickle-style headstock, but without the hook on the lower bout. Originally, the controls were mounted from the front on a black powder-coated control plate, but were later mounted from the rear.

L-5000

The L-5000, introduced in 1987, was G&L's first five-string bass. Its pickup was an MFD split-coil unit, with one coil for the lower three strings and the other coil for the upper two strings. It had a black powder-coated metal control plate to house the pickups and passive controls, just as on the SB-1, but the knobs were chromed metal instead of the SB-1's plastic. The L-5000 had a sickle-style headstock and narrow string spacing due to its use of a 1¾-inch nut width (same as the four-string basses at the time). This was one of the reasons it was discontinued around 1993.

ASAT Bass/ASAT Bass Signature

The ASAT bass was introduced in 1989 and was basically a repackaged L-2000. The most visible difference was the Telecaster (ASAT) body shape and the slim neck (1½-inch nut width) profile reminiscent of a Jazz bass. We thought it would be interesting to make a bass in a Tele shape, and several people told us we should put it into production. The trouble was that the bass became neck-heavy because of the smaller body shape and lack of an upper horn to provide leverage for a strap. Our solution was to use a slim profile neck, which weighed less than the 1¾-inch nut width neck.

In 1989, we introduced a Leo Fender signature version, which was the same in all respects except for the signature decal on the body.

Chapter 28

G&L in the '90s: The Second Decade

The biggest news for both G&L and musicians everywhere at the start of the '90s was Leo's death on March 21, 1991. Since Leo and his life's work had touched so many people around the world, it seemed appropriate for G&L to produce some kind of special tribute to him. The beautiful Commemorative guitar and bass models were the result.

Commemorative Guitar

The Commemorative guitar was made in 1991. It was basically an ASAT Classic with cosmetic enhancements, including a cherryburst-finished swamp ash body with top binding, a bound flame maple neck and gold-plated metal parts, including pickguard and pole pieces. Even the strings were gold-plated. The headstock had a Commemorative decal in place of the ASAT Classic decal, while the body had a decal of Leo Fender's signature with the years of his life below it, 1909-1991. Below the years was a rose with gold petals. There were also about seven Commemoratives made with an Australian Lacewood top and back with a natural gloss finish.

We planned to make 1,000 Commemorative guitars, as the neck plates were numbered 1 of 1,000 and so on. However, Fender's lawsuit against G&L regarding the use of Leo Fender's name on the instrument moved aggressively following Leo's death. The suit claimed this created confusion in the marketplace between Fender and G&L products. It was up to BBE Sound's management to settle the matter. BBE reluctantly agreed to stop using Leo's name on the instruments, so unfortunately, the special Commemorative model was cut short, to about 250. Replacement gold neck plates were issued to reflect the smaller total number of Commemorative guitars.

Commemorative Bass

The Commemorative bass was a cosmetically enhanced ASAT bass. It had a cherryburst-finished swamp ash body, flame maple neck and gold-plated parts including the strings. The same Commemorative headstock and body decals were used. Like the production of the guitar, production of the bass was cut short due to the settlement of the Fender lawsuit. Only about 150 were made.

Chapter 29
Evolution of the ASAT

ASAT Classic

Throughout the '90s, the ASAT Classic continued largely unchanged, except for a few details. The pickguard went from white powder-coated metal to three-ply white plastic. There were several optional pickguards, including black, pearl and tortoiseshell.

Near the end of the '90s, G&L offered three-ply crème as well as a one-ply black for a vintage appearance, which worked especially well on the Butterscotch Blonde finish introduced at about the same time. In the late '90s, the standard body wood became alder, with swamp ash as an upgrade option.

The Leo Fender signature version of the ASAT Classic was discontinued at the same time the Commemorative production was stopped.

ASAT Classic Custom

In 1996, the ASAT Classic Custom was introduced. It had a bird's eye maple neck with a choice of maple or rosewood fingerboard, a swamp ash top over an

G&L 20th-Anniversary model; 1 of 50. (PG)

Neck plate of 20th-anniversary ASAT; 1 of 50. (PG)

alder body, wood binding, rear body contour, a pearl pickguard, and came with a deluxe Tolex case. In all other regards, the ASAT Classic Custom was the same as the standard ASAT Classic. This model was short-lived. All the features that made this model different became options that could be mixed and matched on any ASAT Classic.

ASAT Standard and ASAT Special

In about 1993, the ASAT was split into two models, the ASAT Standard and ASAT Special. The ASAT Standard continued with the powder-coated black hardware (bridge, control plate,

knobs, and tuners), along with the black pickup covers. The black powder-coated metal pickguard gave way to a three-ply plastic one, but optional pickguards were offered just as on the ASAT Classic. The ASAT Standard's body wood became alder instead of swamp ash.

The ASAT Special, on the other hand, came with a swamp ash body and all chrome hardware, as on the ASAT Classic Signature model. The ASAT Special's standard pickguard was three-ply white, which it remains today. All the same pickguard choices were offered.

1990 ASAT Classic with "Leo Fender" decal. (PG)

ASAT Special in goldflake with gun-oil tinted neck. (PG)

ASAT Deluxe and ASAT Custom

In early 1996, the ASAT Deluxe and ASAT Custom were introduced at the Winter NAMM Show. The ASAT Deluxe was unlike any other ASAT in that it had two Seymour Duncun humbuckers—a '59N in the neck position and a TB-4 in the bridge position. The ASAT Deluxe also had a figured maple top over a mahogany body, rear-mounted controls, white top binding, and bird's eye maple neck with choice of maple or rosewood fingerboard. Controls consisted of a three-position pickup selector, volume and tone.

About one year later, a mini-toggle switch was added to allow coil splitting of both pickups.

The ASAT Custom was basically the same as the ASAT Deluxe except it used the MFD single-coil pickups from the ASAT Special. This model was almost immediately discontinued, with back orders from around the time of the NAMM Show being filled until May 1996. Total production of the ASAT Custom was only about 17 pieces.

1999 ASAT speical edition, #1 of 20, designed by Buffalo Brothers.

ASAT Special Semi-Hollow

ASAT Z-3

The ASAT Z-3 was introduced in 1998, though over the years several examples of such a guitar had been built, particularly for artists such as John Jorgenson. Its official introduction didn't come as a surprise for G&L fans, who had waited about eight years.

ASAT Semi-Hollow and ASAT Classic Semi-Hollow

The most important evolution of the ASAT and ASAT Classic came in 1998, with the introduction of the ASAT Semi-Hollow and ASAT Classic Semi-Hollow. Even though dealers and sales reps sometimes referred to them as "thinlines," they were different from the Fender Telecaster Thinline guitars. The G&Ls were true semi-hollow bodies, with chambers on both sides. The Fenders had a chamber on one side and a routed control cavity on the other, which was covered by

Photo courtesy of Tim Page

ASAT Classic Thinline

Photo courtesy of Tim Page

ASAT Thinline with Bigsby vibrato.

pickguard mounted controls. The G&L Semi-Hollow models' tone had a less pronounced midrange, which accentuated the lows and highs.

Semi-hollow versions of the ASAT Z-3 and ASAT Deluxe appeared in 1998 as well. The ASAT Z-3 Semi-Hollow had the same sort of scooped midrange, giving it a distinctively different sound from the ASAT Z-3 and Comanche. The ASAT Deluxe Semi-Hollow gained a smoother overall tone and was capable of tones similar to a jazz guitar.

133

Chapter 30
Evolution of the S-500 and Comanche

Modern S-500

The modern S-500 continued throughout the '90s virtually unchanged, with the exception of the standard body wood becoming alder instead of swamp ash in about 1997. The modern S-500 has a volume control, and treble cut and bass cut controls, which work on all three pickups.

This is unlike a Stratocaster's two tone controls for treble cut only, with one of them working on the neck pickup and the other on the middle pickup. The G&L arrangement on the S-500 became known as the PTB, or Passive Treble Bass, system in about 1991.

Legacy

In 1992, the Legacy debuted. It was based on the S-500 but had vintage style Alnico 5 non-staggered pole pieces. The Legacy doesn't have the S-500's mini-toggle switch, locking tuners or chrome metal knobs, but uses traditional plastic Strat knobs. The standard body wood is alder. The Legacy was basically a result of dealers asking for a G&L with all the hand craftsmanship

Legacy flame-top

Legacy with gold hardware

and technical improvements (Dual-Fulcrum vibrato, Bi-Cut neck, PTB system, etc.) By dropping some of the high-cost parts of the S-500, such as the locking tuners, swamp ash body, and the MFD pickups, the Legacy came in at an aggressive price-point attractive to dealers. Although the price of the Legacy has gone up quite a bit over the years, the Legacy was G&L's best-selling model until recently.

Legacy Special

The Legacy Special was targeted at the player who wanted a hot single-coil sound. It accomplished this through the use of three dual-blade, single-coil humbuckers. The neck and middle were called Dual Blade, while the hotter bridge pickup was called a Power Blade. It was like the Legacy in most other respects, except for having a Graph-Tech self-lubricating nut, as well as locking tuners and a swamp ash body.

Legacy Special with dual-blade pickups. (PG)

George Fullerton Signature Model

This model, introduced in 1996, is the closest thing to a 1959 Stratocaster ever made by G&L. It is like a Legacy, but even more vintage in design. It has a vintage Strat control configuration and is wired entirely with cotton pushback wire insulation. It also has a swamp ash body, late '50s-style soft "V" neck profile and vintage-style small frets.

Like the Leo Fender Signature models, the George Fullerton Signature model has my signature in a decal on the body. However, the model also has my signature on the headstock and a special serial number system, which started with GF0001 stamped into the chrome neck plate. Each guitar comes with an autographed copy of my book, *Guitar Legends*. The guitar was originally shipped in a deluxe tweed case, but that was changed to a deluxe Tolex case in 2000.

Modern Comanche

After a hiatus of about eight years, the Comanche returned in 1998. This was essentially the Comanche V repackaged in modern S-500 trim. Beside the pickups, the difference between the modern S-500 and the modern Comanche is that the Comanche has a Graph-Tech self-lubricating nut and offers a choice of swamp ash or alder body wood depending on the chosen finish.

136

Chapter 31
Evolution of G&L Rock Guitars

Climax Line

In 1993, the Climax line was introduced with three models having different pickup configurations. The Climax had two Alnico magnet single-coils in the neck and middle positions, and a G&L traditional humbucker in the bridge position. The Climax XL had two such G&L humbuckers, and the Climax Plus had the two humbuckers and an Alnico single-coil in the middle position.

All Climax guitars came with swamp ash bodies, Floyd Rose locking vibratos and slim, fast playing necks. Controls were simple—one volume and one tone control, and either a five-position (Climax and Climax Plus) or three-position (Climax XL) pickup selector. The body shape was like Jackson's double cutaway models, without the soft edges of most G&L models. The Climax line was discontinued a couple of years later.

Invader Line

After a year or so hiatus from the rock guitar market, G&L returned with the Invader line in 1997. Once again, there were three-pickup-combination choices, labeled just like the Climax line—Invader, Invader XL, and Invader Plus. The pickups were different, however. The Invader had two blade-type humbuckers from the Legacy Special, with a Seymour Duncan TB-4 humbucker in the bridge position. The Invader XL had a Seymour Duncan '59N humbucker in the neck position and a TB-4 in the bridge position. The Invader Plus had the '59N and TB-4 humbuckers, with the blade-type middle humbucker from the Legacy Special.

Like the Climax guitars, all standard Invader models had Floyd Rose locking vibratos, swamp ash bodies, one volume and one tone control, and either a five-position (Invader and Invader Plus) or three-position (Invader XL) pickup selector. The difference was that the Invader models included a mini-toggle switch to split the coils of the Seymour Duncan humbucker(s). Also, Invader models could be ordered with either the Dual-Fulcrum vibrato or Saddle-Lock bridge in place of the Floyd Rose vibrato. All Invader models came with a deluxe Tolex case.

There were also deluxe versions of all three Invader models, featuring figured maple tops over mahogany bodies, natural wood binding, and bird's eye maple necks. Next to the Commemorative model, these were some of the most expensive G&L guitars ever offered.

Chapter 32
G&L Basses in the '90s

L-2000 and ASAT Bass

Both of these models continued unchanged until about 1998, when the standard body wood became alder instead of swamp ash. The L-2000 had some additional modifications, including a change to a six-bolt neck attachment with countersunk ferrules instead of a neck plate. At the same time, the L-2000's body perimeter was trimmed 1/32 of an inch, except the waistline, which was trimmed even further.

L-5500

The L-5500 was G&L's second five-string bass, but this one was designed as a five-string from scratch, while the L-5000 was more a modified four-string. The L-5500 had EMG DC40s with EMG preamp, a wider neck than the four-string bass and a six-bolt neck attachment with neck plate. Despite having a great review in *Bass Player* magazine, the dealers and the public made it clear that what they really wanted from G&L was a five-string L-2000.

ASAT bass, 1991, without Leo Fender decal. (PG)

ASAT Semi-Hollow bass (PG)

L-2500

The five-string L-2500 was introduced almost 17 years after the L-2000. The L-5500 was discontinued and replaced with the L-2500. Still, the L-2500 was heavily revised within two years. The body wood changed from solid swamp ash to lighter weight tilia with a swamp ash top. The neck shape and dimensions were new, the headstock changed to its current 3+2 tuning machine arrangement, and the body underwent similar changes to the L-2000's. Though the original version of the L-2500 used a six-bolt neck attachment

with neck plate, the revised L-2500 used a six-bolt neck attachment with the same countersunk string ferrule system as on other G&L basses.

Custom Versions

In about 1995, G&L offered so-called Custom versions (L-2000 Custom, etc.) of the L-2000 and L-5500 basses. These had flat tops without arm contours, wood binding, bird's eye maple necks, and came with deluxe Tolex cases. The body wood was alder with a swamp ash top, sort of a precursor to the evolution of the L-2500.

First prototype Semi-Hollow ASAT bass (PG)

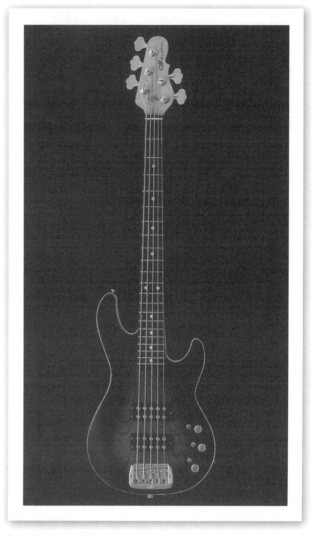

L-2500 5-string bass

L-1500 and L-1505

The L-1500 and L-1505 brought back G&L's tradition of single humbucker basses, as in the L-1000. However, the L-1500 four-string and L-1505 five-string are decidedly different. Both are active basses, with preamp and electronics similar to those in the L-2000 and L-2500, but without the pickup selector switch and treble boost position on the preamp control. (These were already quite bright sounding.) Though neither the L-1500 or L-2500 sell as well as their two-pickup counterparts, they have found a good niche in the market.

Legacy Bass/LB-100

The Legacy bass was introduced in 1992 along with the Legacy guitar. Like the Legacy guitar concept, the Legacy bass mated a vintage Alnico pickup with G&L's technical improvements and handmade quality.

However, the Legacy bass ran into two obstacles. First, bass manufacturer Zon already had a bass called the Legacy, so our bass was renamed LB-100. Second, dealers and players did not want a vintage-style Precision bass from G&L—they wanted G&L's progressive designs instead. The

L-2500 5-string fretless bass (PG)

L-1500 bass

vintage/modern concept worked brilliantly in the Legacy guitar line but failed miserably in the Legacy bass line, despite some heavyweight stars such as INXS bassist Garry Beers praising the LB-100 as being better than his most prized vintage Precision basses. Consequently, the LB-100 was finally discontinued toward the end of the '90s.

SB-1 and SB-2

Both of these models continued unchanged in the '90s. But the SB-1 was discontinued in the late '90s due to slow sales. The SB-2 was not changed to the six-bolt neck attachment, but remained with a three-bolt neck plate arrangement.

L-1505 5-string bass

Chapter 33

Creating the Custom Creations Department

On June 15, 1998, G&L opened its Custom Creations Department. The goal was to make limited-edition instruments with distinctive tonal and visual characteristics separate from traditional handcrafted G&L instruments. A select team of our most experienced craftsmen was chosen to produce the instruments.

Each instrument produced by the G&L Custom Creations Department includes special documentation, both in certificate form and on the instrument itself. Special hand-marked identification bearing the model name, the number produced, date of instrument completion, and signature of the G&L plant manager appear on the rear of the headstock, with corresponding identification discreetly located on the body itself. A certificate included shows all of the information found on the instrument, as well as details about the origin of concept, purpose and distinctive features.

"We hope these special instruments produced by the G&L Custom Creations Department will stir the hearts, minds and souls of discerning musicians who are fortunate enough to acquire them," said BBE Sound President John McLaren, when the department was founded.

ASAT Classic III

In April 1998, the G&L artist program requested an ASAT Classic with a third, centrally located pickup and five-position selector switch. A reverse-wound ASAT Classic neck pickup was requested for the middle position, but tooling to reverse-wind this pickup was not yet in existence. The new Custom Creations Department responded by developing tooling to allow the ASAT Classic neck pickup to be reverse-wound. Thus, the ASAT Classic III was born as the first limited-edition instrument from the G&L Custom Creations Department. There were only 100 built. Here are the specifications for the ASAT Classic III.

BODY WOOD:	Swamp ash, top bound
BODY FINISH:	Three-tone sunburst
NECK WOOD:	Bird's eye maple
NECK FINISH:	Hand-rubbed gun-oil tint with polished gloss finish
NECK WIDTH:	1 5/8" width at nut
NECK RADIUS:	7 1/2"
FRETWIRE:	Medium Jumbo 6100
TUNERS:	Schaller
NECK PICKUP:	Standard ASAT Classic
PICKGUARD:	Three-ply pearl
MIDDLE PICKUP:	Reverse-wound classic neck
CASE:	Tolex hardshell
BRIDGE PICKUP:	Standard ASAT Classic
CONTROLS:	Five-way selector, volume, tone

Listing the specs doesn't do anything to capture what really makes this guitar special. The unbelievable tones this guitar creates have to be heard to be believed.

ASAT Junior

In February 1998, prior to the formation of the Custom Creations Department, G&L was experimenting using mahogany bodies with various MFD pickups. The new department continued experimenting and developed the ASAT Junior, a unique and beautiful instrument. Kalamazoo-inspired elements were incorporated into both the appearance and tonal composition, and blended with the unmistakable tones of the MFD ASAT pickups. Below are the specifications for the ASAT Junior, the second limited edition instrument produced by the G&L Custom Creations Department. There were only 250 built.

BODY WOOD:	Chambered mahogany
BODY FINISH:	Translucent cherry
NECK WOOD:	Mahogany with ebony fingerboard
NECK FINISH:	Translucent cherry
NECK WIDTH:	1 5/8" width at nut
NECK RADIUS:	12"
FRETWIRE:	Medium Jumbo 6100
TUNERS:	Chrome Schaller
NECK PICKUP:	Custom ASAT Special with black covers
PICKGUARD:	Three-ply black LP-style
BRIDGE PICKUP:	Custom ASAT Special with black covers
CASE:	Tolex hardshell
BRIDGE:	Stop-bar tailpiece
CONTROLS:	Rear mounted; three-way LP-style selector, volume, tone; black LP-style knobs

The concept for the ASAT Junior really started because many players new to the ASAT Special mistook its large, rectangular MFD pickups for P-90 pickups. Naturally, we explained that the pickups were not P-90s, but different in design. However, we wanted to have fun with the idea that ASAT Special pickups have a similar appearance to P-90s. The styling influences for the ASAT Junior are obvious, but the tone is unlike anything that came from Kalamazoo. After all, the heart of the ASAT Junior is its real ASAT Special MFD pickups.

The ASAT Junior debuted at the 1998 Summer NAMM Show in Nashville. The crowd was knocked out. Word of this guitar got around the show rapidly. Many Nashville gunslingers drooled over the cool look of the guitar, but when they plugged it in, they couldn't believe the tones. "The clean tones are the best!" we heard. "No way, dirty that thing up, and it's even better!" commented another. This guitar kicked some serious butt, and everyone knew it.

Photo courtesy of Tim Page

Limited-edition ASAT Junior (PG)

146

Chapter 34

G&L in the New Millennium

Most guitar models remain the same, including the ASAT, Legacy, S-500, Comanche, and Invader models. However, some new models were added. All the G&L basses in production at the end of the '90s continued into the new millennium unchanged. There was one addition to the line.

ASAT Classic Bluesboy and ASAT Classic Bluesboy Semi-Hollow

The ASAT Classic Bluesboy was first produced as a limited edition for G&L dealer Buffalo Brothers of California. Tim Page co-owns the store with his brother, Bob. Tim handles electric instruments while Bob looks after acoustics. Tim wanted to do a version of the ASAT Classic with a traditional humbucker in the neck position, and Seymour Duncan stepped in to recommend its traditional PAF humbucker, the Seth Lover model. Testing conducted by both G&L and Tim concluded that the Seth Lover neck pickup was an excellent choice to pair with the ASAT Classic's MFD single coil. Buffalo Brothers commissioned the lim-

2001 Bluesboy

Bluesboy special edition, #1 of 20, designed by Buffalo Brothers.

ited run of ASAT Classic Bluesboy guitars, with the name Bluesboy being Tim's idea. The guitar was so well received by Buffalo Brothers' clientele that Tim persuaded G&L to introduce both solid body and semi-hollow versions.

ASAT Special Deluxe and S-500 Deluxe

At the 2002 Winter NAMM Show, G&L introduced deluxe versions of the ASAT Special and S-500. These models include figured maple tops over basswood bodies, with rear-mounted controls and no pickguard to cover up the beautiful

wood. In all other respects, these models are the same as the standard versions.

ASAT Classic Custom

Also at 2002 Winter NAMM Show, the ASAT Classic Custom name was revived, but for an entirely different instrument. The 2002 ASAT Classic Custom is like the standard ASAT Classic in all respects except for the neck pickup. The concept began by taking the ASAT Special's neck pickup and installing it on an ASAT Classic, but from there the concept evolved into a quest to make the biggest, fattest-sounding single-coil

MFD neck pickup ever made by G&L. The pickup was designed to come close to the warmth and fatness of the PAF, but retain the brighter top end and chiming harmonics of a single coil. In essence, the guitar was to bridge the sonic gap between the ASAT Classic and the Bluesboy.

To do this, G&L experimented with different winds on the stock ASAT Special's neck pickup bobbin, but the final version used longer pole pieces, which allowed a wider bobbin aperture. This allowed not only more winds, but also made them stack up differently. The result is the ASAT Classic Custom, which is really a great guitar for blues and bluesy rock.

JB-2

Some of the most influential bass dealers in the United States told G&L that there was room in the market for another vintage/modern effort,

Geoff Fullerton and Tim Page talking about guitars.

Tim and Bob Page, the "Buffalo Brothers": the world's largest G&L dealer.

Tim Page, Georg Fullerton, and Marc Burroughs (back to camera): just talking guitars.

George Fullerton and Tim Page: George is signing Tim's guitar.

Tim Page and George Fullerton.

this time a Jazz-type bass. Since G&L was not successful with the LB-100, it took some convincing to make the new bass. Once again, the formula was simple: Take the tried-and-true four-string L-2000 and mate it with traditional Alnico jazz pickups and passive electronics. Dealers told G&L that the Jazz market was hot, unlike the Precision bass market, and many customers who wanted a Jazz-type bass were forced to choose instruments from other manufacturers. They wanted the familiar feel of their G&Ls and the technical benefits of the Saddle-Lock bridge and Ultra-Lite tuners, combined with a vintage sound. The resulting bass, the JB-2, is selling well and has received glowing reviews from *Bass Player* and other magazines.

JB-2 bass (PG)

Chapter 35
Distinctive G&L Features

There are four elements that distinguish a G&L instrument from other instruments. Here are details on each innovation.

Magnetic Field Design (MFD) Pickups

The patented Magnetic Field Design (MFD) pickups use a ceramic bar magnet installed underneath each coil, with soft iron adjustable pole pieces to transfer the magnetic field to the surface of the pickup. By contrast, traditional Alnico pickups, such as those in the Legacy and George Fullerton models, use nonadjustable Alnico pole pieces, leaving pickup height as the only adjustment. The MFD pickups have this adjustment, but also offer individual adjustment of each pole piece, letting the player effectively adjust the output of each string on each pickup. MFD pickups yield about twice the output per wind, making the pickup quieter while allowing a greater overall output. The sound of MFD pickups is slightly warmer with a broader frequency response.

One major Nashville session guitarist remarked that the G&L S-500 with MFD pickups sounded as balanced and "sweet" as his favorite old vintage Alnico equipped axe. The difference is that the S-

500 sounds good right into his amp without all the EQ tweaking of his mixing console that made his other guitar sound good. When he ran his S-500 though his studio rig, he was truly amazed at the rich and warm, yet clear and sparkly sound.

Dual-Fulcrum Vibrato

The patented Dual-Fulcrum vibrato was designed to be the best unit in the music business. The heavy steel bridge plate has two holes on the front edge countersunk on each side halfway through the metal. Where the countersinks meet, a knife-edge is created that fits into a V-shaped groove in the mounting post. The steel mounting post is threaded on the lower end to screw into a heavy brass insert pressed into the body. A V-shaped groove is cut into the post near the upper end. The post's top is larger to prevent plate slippage and features a hole so an Allen wrench can raise and lower the plate. After the steel parts are completed, they are case-hardened before plating. This prevents wear on the knife-edge. The friction-free action is much smoother and thus superior to the six screws that mount vintage tremolos. Each note's tone is changed higher or lower as the plate is moved, unlike vintage tremolos. The machined aluminum handle is ¼-inch diameter, which is stronger than handles used on vintage models. The handle holder is mounted on the plate in a hole that has a flat side to prevent the part from turning. The holder has a threaded hole on the side with a nylon insert under a setscrew that applies pressure to prevent the handle from being too loose or tight. The bridge saddles are fully adjustable for perfect string intonation. The strings are brought from the back through the heavy block and bridge plate. In 2001, G&L improved the saddle design by replacing the die-cast units with billet brass-machined saddles.

Saddle-Lock Bridge

The solid-body electric guitar does not primarily get its sound from the body. The strings vibrating in the magnetic field create the signal sent to the amplifier to make the sound. That's why the patented Saddle-Lock bridge used on G&L instruments is so revolutionary.

The most significant feature of the Saddle-Lock bridge is a small Allen screw on its side, which presses all the saddles together so they resonate as though they were one single mass. This eliminates the loss of string vibration energy caused by side-to-side saddle movement inherent in other designs. Further, the strings no longer need to be routed though the rear of the body for optimum sustain, but now enter directly through the rear of the bridge. For G&L five-string basses, the Saddle-Lock bridge is designed to allow strings to be inserted through the rear of the bridge or rear of the body. G&L found that the increased break angle on the low B string yielded a more focused sound when routed through the rear of the body.

The bottom side of the Saddle-Lock bridge has a large protrusion, which fits into a routed-out spot in the body. The protrusion fits snugly against the end grain of the body wood, allowing the highly resonant bridge to transfer much more of the string vibration energy directly to the core of the body, yielding much greater sustain than Leo's earlier fixed bridge design. Again, Leo's innovative Saddle-Lock design was used to minimize string breakage.

In 2001, G&L improved the design by replacing the die-cast units with billet brass-machined saddles, further improving tone and sustain.

Bi-Cut Neck

Although Leo did not use this approach in the early days, the patented Bi-Cut neck was a great invention that improved the installation of truss rods. The traditional method of truss rod installation involves routing out the back of the neck, installing the truss rod, and covering the spot with a rosewood stripe commonly referred to as a "skunk stripe." Another traditional installation routs the spot for the truss rod on the face of the neck, covering it with the fingerboard.

In contrast, the Bi-Cut method involves cutting the neck blank in half longitudinally, routing the inside, inserting the truss rod, and gluing the two halves together. Thin tubing is placed over the rod to protect it from the glue. The completed neck blank is then put in a Taylor press with approximately 350 pounds of pressure, assuring a nearly invisible truss rod installation. The Bi-Cut method achieves exceptional resistance to warping and twisting, because the centrally located glue joint is actually stronger than the wood on either side. Other manufacturers cannot use this superior type of neck construction because G&L holds the patent exclusively.

PART IV
Favorite Players and Entertainers

Chapter 36
The Importance of Classic Cowboys

Manufacturing Fender and G&L instruments brought Leo and I in contact with many interesting and talented people we considered great friends. These wonderful people are spread out across the country. I hope you'll indulge me as I share some wonderful memories about the contributions of these musicians.

Leo and I always had particular respect and gratitude for the people of Nashville, Tenn., and of the Grand Ole Opry. In the early days, a large part of our business was working with country musicians. I remember the old Ryman Auditorium and the pleasure it brought to so many. Even today a large segment of the music world is centered in Nashville.

There are many fine musical genres associated with the Nashville scene. They include gospel, country, bluegrass, country rock, blues, and western swing. Other crossover genres are pop, rock, jazz, and cowboy western music.

However, I prefer to call all of these "American music," because they add much to our heritage.

Bob Wills

The importance of these musicians to increasing the popularity of the guitar cannot be overstated. The romantic image of cowboys strumming on guitars stays with us to this day.

Leo had special friends in the music business. One of these was Bob Wills and the Texas Playboys. Their western swing band provided many years of beautiful songs and dance music. Bob wrote and recorded "Faded Love," which was always one of Leo's favorites. Bob and the Texas Playboys played at most of the rodeos held in the Midwest, but their base was Caines Academy in Tulsa, Okla. This is where they had a daily radio broadcast for many years.

In addition to being associated with cowboy musicians, we had the privilege of meeting several movie cowboys who also sang. Unfortunately, many have passed on, and with them went symbols of a good way of life. Their clean shows were suitable for family viewing, but that kind of movie is slipping away. At the same time, their warm way of singing and playing music is disappearing as well.

Leo and I became friends with many of these great people including Roy Rogers, Dale Evans, Gene Autry, and Eddie Dean. They will be missed by young people who didn't have the opportunity to enjoy their music and work on the silver screen.

Roy Rogers and Dale Evans—This pair was special to Leo and I since we always appreciated the good things they stood for. Roy Rogers started his musical career in the 1920s. His real name was Leonard Franklin Slye. After coming to California from Ohio in 1930, he began his singing career in Hollywood. He met two other men who were try-

ing to get started as singers. Roy formed the Pioneer Trio with these two men: Bob Nolan and Tim Spencer. When it became necessary to add

Sons of the Pioneers onstage in Tucson, Arizona.

George Fullerton and Dale Warren, Trail Boss for Sons of the Pioneers.

Sunny Spencer, Lucille Fullerton, and Luther Nallie (Sons of the Pioneers).

Roy Rogers with his golden palomino, "Trigger."

more members to the group, they became the Sons of the Pioneers. They were the best known group of singing cowboys in the area.

George Fullerton with the Sons of the Pioneers in Tucson, Arizona.

Sunny Spencer of the Sons of the Pioneers playing his G&L guitar.

Gary LeMaster of the Sons of the Pioneers playing his new special Custom Color G&L guitar.

In 1937, Roy auditioned for Republic Pictures. After he started to work for Republic, his movie name was Dick Weston. Within one year, his name was changed back to Roy Rogers, when he teamed up with his golden palomino, Trigger. He was well on his way to becoming "King of the Cowboys."

He used his singing group, the Sons of the Pioneers, in many of his movies. In 1944, he started working with his leading lady, Dale Evans. Having lost his first wife, Roy and Dale were married in 1947. Over the period of many years, Roy and his beloved bride rode together in 28 movies. In particular, I cherish the movie "The Cowboy and the Senorita." In it, the "King of the Cowboys" and his "Queen of the West" rode the happy trails together. Dale wrote the song, "Happy Trails." Roy and Dale will always be remembered for their wonderful life together and their strong faith in God.

Gene Autry—Leo and I were not as closely associated with Gene Autry, but we counted him as a friend and a big part of the music and entertainment business. Gene was called "America's Favorite Cowboy." On his horse named

Sunny Spencer and Gary LeMaster of the Sons of the Pioneers playing their G&L ASAT guitars.

Gene Autry, "America's Favorite Cowboy."

Champion, he rode through Western movies for many years. He was a favorite cowboy star in the Saturday matinees. He wore the white hat and won hearts as he sang love songs and played his

Eddie Dean's star on the "Walk of Fame" (Palm Springs, CA).

Eddie Dean and George Fullerton at Eddie's birthday party, held at the Iverson Ranch, where most of Eddie's movies were made. This was the last time I saw Eddie; he passed away a few weeks later.

guitar. His talents added greatly to the Western heritage that means so much to all of us. After many years in the movie and business world, he built the wonderful Gene Autry Western Heritage Museum in Los Angeles. Younger people will probably only remember him as the owner of the Angels, a Major League Baseball team in Anaheim, but his fame covers many more phases of life.

Eddie Dean—Eddie Dean, a movie cowboy and his wife, Dearest, were friends with Leo and I for many years. We valued their friendship and sincerely appreciated the great movies Eddie made. He was a cowboy hero of the silver screen. We loved the golden voice of this talented man and the way he strummed his guitar.

Eddie's songs and great singing style earned him the title, "The Golden Cowboy." He will be remembered for keeping the lore of the cowboy and the West alive so that future generations might be proud of our heritage. Eddie was also an avid booster for G&L guitars.

Eddie's manager, Don Bradley, invited me to a birthday party for Eddie at the Iverson Ranch, which was where many of Eddie's movies were filmed. My son Geoff and I attended, and it was great to see so many of Eddie's friends at this special outdoor occasion. The entertainment was great, with bands playing and singers performing. I especially enjoyed the time I spent talking with Eddie. It was the last time I saw him because he passed away a few weeks later.

Eddie Dean, "The Golden Cowboy"

Chapter 37
Contemporary Country Musicians

Our fondness for cowboy musicians extends to the present day. I have had the opportunity to meet several contemporary groups in my travels through the music industry. Here are a few of my memories and comments from these important folks.

Riders in the Sky—From their Harmony Ranch, it's still Woody Paul's dazzling fiddle, Too Slim's madcap sense of humor, and Ranger Doug's golden-throated yodels. Riders in the Sky has been together for more than 20 years and has traveled more than a million miles on the road. This trio has endured with its original lineup intact longer than any other Nashville group. Over the years, nothing changed the basic recipe of this Grand Ole Opry favorite.

In addition to their original compositions, they feature the classics of Gene Autry, Roy Rogers, Bob Wills, Tex Ritter, and the Sons of the Pioneers. Rounder Records released Riders in the Sky's first record in 1980. The group returned to Rounder Records in 1995 with "The Trail Tip Song: Always Drink Upstream From the Herd."

Riders in the Sky: Woody Paul, Ranger Doug, Too Slim.

Riders in the Sky has Christmas, children's, and comedy albums. It also released *Public Cowboy #1: The Music of Gene Autry*, a tribute album. The collection salutes the man who was first to popularize the singing cowboy image.

The group has earned awards from various organizations for its dedication to Western music. Riders in the Sky won two Wrangler statuettes at the 35th-annual Western Heritage Awards at the National Cowboy Hall of Fame in Oklahoma City.

"It's just three guys who do what they love," says Ranger Doug. An album review in People magazine referred to Ranger Doug as "just possibly the world's greatest living yodeler."

Riders in the Sky has appeared in movies, has its own line of Western merchandise and a Web site. All of this is dedicated to keeping the cowboy image and Western heritage alive. This trio is truly a remarkable American original. Their motto is, "It's the Cowboy Way."

Jo Dee Messina—Jo Dee Messina is a top star in Nashville. When she was 12 years old, she discovered country music, including Alabama, The Judds, Janie Fricke, Deborah Allen, and Reba McEntire, and her course was set.

Messina recalls, "I won the grand prize in a talent contest and part of the deal was getting to sing on a live radio broadcast from Kentucky." She became a regular on the show.

166

Michael Martin Murphey

Later she went to Fanfare as Tim McGraw's guest. There she met Curb A&R executive Phil Gernhard backstage. Before long, Messina was in the studio with Byron Gallimore and Tim McGraw, co-producing her debut album. It came out of the chute hotter than Georgia asphalt, and a star was born. Her band members Ralph Friedrichsen and Tony Obrohta use a G&L ASAT guitar and a G&L L-2000 bass.

Michael Martin Murphey—As a boy, Michael Martin Murphey fanticized about being a cowboy. Later he focused his dreams on singing cowboy songs. All things Western motivate him. He has earned many awards for his songs. His song, "Land of Enchantment," became a New Mexico state ballad in 1989. Many leading artists such as Nitty Gritty Dirt Band, Johnny Lee, Jerry Jeff Walker, The Monkees, Kenny Rogers, and John Denver have recorded his songs.

Michael was influenced by Marty Robbins, Buffalo Bill Cody, and other singing cowboys. He visited Roy Rogers and asked the legendary entertainer what things he thought contributed to his success. Roy told Michael it was important to sing from a horse. He said a lot of cowboy singers made the mistake of appearing a long way from the ranch and a horse.

Michael said, "I decided to take him up on that and started doing a show on horseback. I've found that Rogers was right. It's the most powerful way of communicating with music."

Michael has made a real effort to support the cowboy image and keep Western things alive. As part of that, he performs at Westfest, a festival honoring the art, music and culture of the old and new West.

Michael said, "It's a tremendous jam session and gathering of entrepreneurs who are interested in Western history." Vince Gill, Clint Black, Pam Tillis, and others who really care about Western heritage have played at Westfest.

Singer/songwriter Suzy Bogguss, a frequent Westfest performer, said: "Since we don't have as many real cowboys as we used to, we need to keep that healthy Western attitude and apply it to every day life."

She said, "Westfest lets you find your own way to walk, to see the beautiful sides of life in nature and in people, instead of buying into all the negativity and anger in the world. The cowboy fantasy is certainly there, but it's also a way of thinking."

Sons of the San Joaquin—Sons of the San Joaquin are excellent entertainers and truly Western gentlemen. The Hannah boys—Lon, Jack, and Joe—were raised on pioneer music and Christian hymns. These two sources, one secular and the other spiritual, shaped their lives. So did their home—the San Joaquin Valley, a fertile land of farms and cattle ranches. They were enamored with the cowboy way of life, which led them to become Western singers.

All three men had successful careers in education, but they put them on hold to follow their fascination with cowboy songs. Their role model was the Sons of the Pioneers, a group started by Roy Rogers. They were impressed with the songs of Bob Nolan and Tim Spencer.

Jack is the group's songwriter and rhythm guitar player. His wonderful composition, "Great

Sons of San Joaquin: Lonnie Hannah, Jack Hannah, and Joe Hannah.

American Cowboy," brought the band much attention. Lon plays lead guitar and Joe plays the bass fiddle. "It's something to keep my hands busy," Joe says. Sometimes the Hannahs have others sit in and play with them. Their well-rounded arrangements have helped them become a leading group in California.

James L. Mapson—Jim is a self-taught luthier. Many of his ideas come from studying what is published in books and various seminars. He has been building guitars since 1995.

Jim is a premier Southern California builder of fine arch-top guitars. He uses the best-quality and appropriate species of wood available. These are very fine hand-crafted jazz guitars.

James L. Mapson: hand-crafted arch-top guitars.

Chapter 38

Travel Tales

Because I'm not working a traditional schedule any longer, my wife and I have been able to attend shows around the country, as well as get acquainted with musicians and entertainers. Our trips were often memorable in that they brought us in contact with people who support the Fender and G&L products that Leo and I designed. Here are a few pages from my travel log.

Branson, MO—We met several important and well-known singers and entertainers in Branson, which has developed into a home for many beau-

Lucille Fullerton, Charley Pride, and George Fullerton in Branson, MO.

tiful theaters. Our friends, Shorty and Marda Robins, took us to see several shows, including Box Car Willie, Charley Pride, Barbara Fairchild, and Glenn Campbell. Shorty plays and loves his G&L guitars.

Nashville, TN—We always enjoy visiting Nashville. We have many friends in this area. On one visit, our friend Dave Kyle invited us to tour

Shorty and Marda Robins with George Fullerton onstage in Branson, MO.

Boxcar Willie and George Fullerton, Branson, MO.

Glenn Campbell onstage in Branson, MO.

George Fullerton and Glenn Campbell.

George Fullerton, Jeff Dayton, and Glenn Campbell. Jeff is Glenn's band leader and guitar player.

the old Ryman Auditorium and to see a stage show about Hank Williams. The original home to the Grand Ole Opry has been restored beautifully, and this show brought back memories of just how spectacular this stage was.

After the show was over, everyone stayed around to greet each other and visit. As special guests, Lucille and I went backstage to meet the stars of

the show and others there to show support. We took photographs with several stars in Minnie Pearl's old dressing room. We were also able to get some pictures on the stage. It was a real treat to have pictures taken front-and-center on the stage where legendary performers have stood.

We also visited the Country Music Hall of Fame and met the people who operate this wonderful establishment. We enjoyed seeing the memorabilia from yesterday's stars, as well as seeing the

George Fullerton, Barbara Fairchild, and Waylon Herron.

Front of the Ryman Auditorium in Nashville, Tennessee.

Waylon Herron and George Fullerton.

Phil Watson and George Fullerton at the front and center stage of the Ryman Auditorium in Nashville, Tennessee.

things associated with the younger, current musicians. In particular, I was pleased to see the Fender double neck steel guitar I donated on display. The guitar belonged to Leon Mcaullife of the Bob Wills band.

During the same trip, Dave took Lucille and I backstage on Saturday night at the Grand Ole Opry. We were guests of Del Reeves, but we also got to see and get aquainted with other top performers. The backstage area contains many dressing rooms for the stars, and most of them are pleased to welcome you in for a visit. From the

Jason Petty, George Lindsay, Grandpa Jones, Phil Watson, and George Fullerton in Minnie Pearl's old dressing room backstage at the old Ryman Auditorium in Nashville, Tennessee.

John Haywood, Louise Mandrell, George Fullerton, and Lucille Fullerton backstage at the old Ryman Auditorium in Nashville, Tennessee.

George Fullerton and Dave Kyle on the stage of the old Ryman Auditorium in Nashville.

Grandpa Jones, George Fullerton, and George Lindsay backstage at the old Ryman Auditorium in Nashville, Tennessee.

George Fullerton, Lucille Fullerton (wearing Captain Lamb's coat and sitting in his chair) with Captain Lamb.

Captain M. Lamb of the General Jackson River Showboat.

The General Jackson River Showboat.

Steve Wariner, Lucille Fullerton, Del Reeves, and George Fullerton backstage at the Grand Ole Opry in Nashville, TN.

George Fullerton, Leon Rhodes, and Eugene Moles backstage at the Grand Ole Opry in Nashville, Tennessee.

George Fullerton, Lucille Fullerton, and Billy Walker backstage at the Grand Ole Opry in Nashville, Tennessee.

Jeannie Pruitt and George Fullerton backstage at the Grand Ole Opry in Nashville, Tennessee.

Little Jimmy Dickens and George Fullerton backstage at the Grand Ole Opry in Nashville, Tennessee.

George Fullerton and Billy Walker backstage at the Grand Ole Opry in Nashville, Tennessee.

The Hager Brothers Twins with George Fullerton backstage at the Grand Ole Opry in Nashville, Tennessee.

George Fullerton, Lucille Fullerton, and Jimmy C. Newman backstage at the Grand Ole Opry in Nashville, Tennessee.

George Fullerton and Buck White of the Whites backstage at the Grand Ole Opry in Nashville, Tennessee.

Rick "L.D." Wayne and George Fullerton backstage at the Grand Ole Opry in Nashville, Tennessee.

Porter Wagoner, Christy Lynn, George Fullerton, and Lucille Fullerton backstage at the Grand Ole Opry in Nashville, Tennessee.

George Fullerton and Johnny Russell backstage at the Grand Ole Opry in Nashville, Tennessee.

Jean Sheppard and George Fullerton backstage at the Grand Ole Opry in Nashville, Tennessee.

Harold Bradley and George Fullerton in Nashville, Tennessee.

George Fullerton and James Freeze backstage at the Grand Ole Opry in Nashville, Tennessee.

Dave Kyle, George Fullerton, Lucille Fullerton, and Fred Newell.

backstage, we could also see the show being performed on stage. It was great to be part of this all-American showplace. Nashville is truly a haven for musicians and entertainers.

Bakersfield, CA—Lucille and I traveled to Bakersfield to visit Buck Owens at his beautiful Crystal Theater. Terry Christoffersen, Buck's manager, met us with a warm welcome. The Crystal Theater is a wonderful and interesting place filled with memorabilia from Buck's long and illustrious career. The theater serves great food and drink each evening before show time. Many traveling musical groups appear at this special place.

After enjoying a wonderful dinner and a terrific show, we went backstage to Buck's office to see

Billy Mize and George Fullerton, Bakersfield, California.

Teddy Spanke, Don Kidwell, and George Fullerton in Bakersfield, California.

George Fullerton and Gene Moles, Bakersfield, California.

Willy Savage and Eugene Moles, Bakersfield, California.

Alvis Barnett, Bonnie Owens, Dennis Payne, Teresa Spanke, and George Fullerton, Bakersfield, California.

him and visit. We had some laughs about the early days at Fender when Buck would visit Leo and I and share news about what was happening

Teddy Spanke and his gold G&L ASAT guitar.

At Trout's Club, the band Tex Pistols (Bob Durham, leader). From left to right: Eugene Moles (red G&L ASAT guitar), Ted Spanke (gold G&L ASAT guitar), Alvis Barnett (drums), Teresa Spanke (singer), Don Kidwell (bass), and Bob Durham (flattop guitar).

Gene Moles, George Fullerton, Dennis Payne, Eugene Moles, and Alvis Barnett.

in the music world. We also reminisced about our many lunches together.

Lucille and I took several pictures with Buck and his manager that night. In particular, I value the one with Buck and I holding the red, white and blue G&L guitar Leo presented to him at the Crazy Horse Steakhouse just a short time before Leo passed away.

During another trip to Bakersfield, Eugene Moles, the guitar player for the Del Reeves Band, invited Lucille and I to come for a special recording session at Buck Owens' old recording studio. Alvis Barnett, drummer for the Del Reeves Band, and Dennis Payne, a guitar player from Nashville, were there as well.

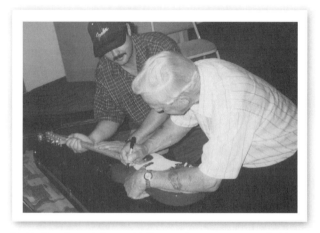

Teddy Spanke and George Fullerton: George is signing Teddy's red G&L ASAT guitar.

Trout's Club in Bakersfield, CA. Ted Spanke is playing a G&L.

We spent a beautiful, sunny day at the recording studio, listening to many people record and even got into some group singing. The recording ended at just about dark. We were pleased to be guests of these great entertainers. We had not met many of them before, but they treated us with great respect and warm acceptance. I spent time signing autographs and guitars—many of them G&Ls.

After the recording session and dinner, we were invited to go with the whole gang of musicians to a club called Trouts for an evening of fun and entertainment. One of the highlights was seeing my old friend, Billy Mize, a well-known singer and entertainer in Southern California, and his wife, Marsha.

The club band was called Tex Pistols, led by Bob Durham. Most musicians from the recording studio joined the regular band for a night of loud music. Eugene Moles and Teddy Spanke were both playing G&L ASAT guitars. Bob played flat-top rhythm guitar. Don Kidwell played a Fender bass and Willie Savage played a Fender guitar. Also Dennis Payne had a '57 Fender Telecaster. Alvis Barnett played drums and Theresa Spanke, Teddy's sister, sang. Bonnie Owens, who works for Merle Haggard, was also at the party. And when the music ended, Lucille and I enjoyed a beautiful hotel room, which was arranged by Inez Savage, a manager of local musical groups.

Victorville, CA—We met Roy "Dusty" Rogers, Jr., who is in charge of operating the Roy Rogers and Dale Evans Museum as chief executive officer of the organization. The museum is a great show place for family history and memorabilia from the

George Fullerton and Bonnie Owens.

Bakersfield, CA: Buck Owens Studio for a recording session— Eugene Moles, Alvis Barnett, and Teresa Spanke.

Roy "Dusty" Rogers, Jr.

silver screen. It also sponsors shows at different times of the year for everyone's musical enjoyment.

Roy "Dusty" Rogers, Jr. and George Fullerton at the Roy Rogers-Dale Evans Museum.

Niles Harper, Roy "Dusty" Rogers, Jr. and George Fullerton at the Roy Rogers-Dale Evans Museum with a special "Roy Rogers" guitar.

Photo courtesy of Dave Kyle

George Fullerton and Marty Stuart at the Roy Rogers-Dale Evans Museum.

Photo courtesy of Dave Kyle

Even though Roy and Dale are gone, their family carries on the musical tradition. Dusty has his own band, the Highland Riders, which plays mostly at local places for special occasions. And Rob Johnson, grandson of Roy and Dale, is the leader of Rob Johnson and Heritage, a contemporary country band and Western act. The group performs at theaters, festivals, and special events. The band has opened for headline performers, such as Steve Wariner, Merle Haggard, Reba McEntire, and Marty Stuart, as well as groups, including the Sons of the Pioneers and the Sons of the San Joaquin.

Heritage is the product of Rob's lifelong love for harmony singing. Rob has been in the music business more than 25 years. He and the band are big boosters for G&L instruments.

Rob Johnson and Heritage: Rob Johnson, his wife Linda, and backup singer Mary Brisend.

Tulsa, OK—We have traveled to the Sooner state to visit Roy and Candy Ferguson, owners and operators of a large music store in Tulsa. They sell G&L guitars as well as Fender guitars and amplifiers. In addition, their band is a popular attraction at the Caines Academy, home of the Bob Wills band. When Roy and Candy sing as a duo, they are known as The Royals.

Huntington Beach, CA—A not-too-distant neighbor to Fullerton, Calif., this beach city is home to our friends Eddie and Shirley Montana. They own and operate a music store, which deals in vintage guitars. Eddie also builds fine custom guitars, called Montana and Murga. In addition, Eddie and Shirley have a musical group that performs in places around California.

Cain's Academy, Tulsa, OK: This was Bob Wills's homebase.

Johnny Lee Wills, (brother of Bob Wills) and Roy Ferguson at Cains Academy.

Eldon Shamblin, lead guitarist for Bob Wills, and Roy Ferguson holding a G&L guitar.

Roy and Candy Ferguson: "The Royals."

Eddie Montana, holding two of his Montana and Murgo guitars.

Eddie and Shirley Montana: she plays a MusicMan bass.

The first Custom guitars built by Montana and Murgo; the black guitar is Eddie's personal instrument.

PART V
Remembering Leo and Recollecting More G&L Details

Chapter 39
Leo's Legacy

The electric guitars and basses that Leo and I designed and produced more than 50 years ago have successfully reached musicians around the globe. That success is still increasing with the popularity of the instruments being built today by G&L. What a wonderful accomplishment from this little town of Fullerton, which became "The Guitar Capital of the World."

The old buildings where this fantastic story began were torn down to make way for other structures, most recently a three-level parking garage. It is unfortunate that the original buildings were not preserved as a historical site to commemorate the invention of solid-body electric guitars and basses. But the accomplishment has not gone unrecognized.

The parking structure has a bronze plaque on the front wall, identifying it as the original Fender factory site, as well as two special murals. The mural on the north side of the structure illustrates the workers in the factory. The mural on the south side pictures the performing artists who use Fender guitars and amplifiers in their music.

185

These murals depict the two groups of people who made the success of Leo's inventions possible.

Guest artist Mike Tauber designed the murals, with assistance by museum staffers Aimee Aul and Andy Elman. Students from local high schools executed the murals under Mike's direction. These students were Becky Bremer, Stephanie Wright, Brittany Boughter, Alex Espinoza, Debora Park, Carly Wellman, and Erin Hornsby.

"Immortalizing Leo" was dedicated in a public ceremony on June 29, 2000. The murals were sponsored by the Fullerton Museum Center and Project CUFFS, a collaboration of education, law enforcement, and community-based organizations to provide at-risk youth with positive alternatives to drugs and gangs.

The day the murals were dedicated many city officials and museum personnel were present. Representatives from G&L and Fender were there,

Street corner of Pomona Ave. and Santa Fe Ave. in Fullerton, California.

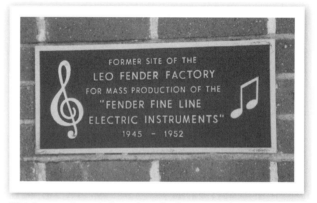

This bronze plaque is located on the front wall of the parking garage at the original Fender factory site.

This parking garage, located at the corner of Pomona Ave. and Santa Fe Ave. in Fullerton, CA, is the location of the first Fender Factory.

Mural on the north side of the structure. (PG)

Mural on the south side of the structure. (PG)

too. People from the news media took pictures and interviewed those in the crowd. A local rock band, Trip the Spring, supplied the music for the dedication. The group played from a second-story balcony above the murals, using all Fender equipment.

After the ceremonies were complete, Joe Felz, the museum director, invited everyone to visit the museum, which is located just a few blocks north on Pomona Ave. Many electric instruments, along with lots of pictures and memorabilia, were on display. It was a happy occasion to see how much everyone cared and enjoyed the success of Leo Fender, a hometown boy who became famous.

When the new Fender museum is completed, it will be a beautiful place to share information and memories with the public. The museum should draw many visitors since the location is near Disneyland, Knott's Berry Farm and the Anaheim

Guest artist Mike Tauber: he was in charge of painting the murals on the parking garage of the old Fender factory.

Aimee Aul from the Leo Fender museum.

Amiee Aul and Alex Espinoza

Artists who painted the murals. Left to right: Mike Tauber, Alex Espinoza, Erin Hornsby, Debora Park, Brittany Bougter, Andy Elman, Aimee Aul, Becky Bremer, Stephanie Wright, and Carly Wellman.

Photos of the murals and the artists courtesy of Aimee Aul, Leo Fender Museum

Convention Center. The Fender museum will be a place where musicians from all over the world will gather together to show their respect for Leo and his contribution to the music industry.

Leo's legacy also lives on at the G&L factory. The leadership of G&L in the guitar business is promising. The company looks forward to many years of carrying on the tradition of crafting handmade instruments for customers. G&L is proud to be part of the continued prosperity of Fullerton, "The Guitar Capital of the World."

Stephanie Wright

Erin Hornsby and Andy Elma

John McLaren, Lucille Fullerton, George Fullerton, and Maureen McLaren

Maureen McLaren and Lucille Fullerton at the dedication of the murals on the building that is located on the site of the first Fender factory, June 29, 2000.

Trip the Spring: the local rock band that supplied the music for the public ceremony "Immortalizing Leo," a dedication of the murals that were painted on the building where the first Fender factory was located, June 29, 2000.

"G&L Guitars and Basses are the best instruments I have ever made."

Leo Fender

Leo Fender with his guitars. Leo says, "These are the best instruments I have ever made."

Photo courtesy of Mrs. Doloris Beard

An aerial view of the east side of Harbor Blvd. in Fullerton, California (population today of approximately 125,000). The number 1 on the building in the upper right portion of the picture is the location of the original Fender Guitar Factory, on the corner of Pomona Ave. and Santa Fe Ave. The number 2 on the building in the picture farther north on Pomona Ave. is the Leo Fender Museum.

An aerial view of the west side of Harbor Blvd. showing Amerige Park, across from the City Hall and Police Department.